OBJECTS

HANS DEICHMANN

.

OBJECTS

A
CHRONICLE
OF
SUBVERSION
IN
NAZI GERMANY
AND
FASCIST ITALY

.

TRANSLATED BY
PETER CONSTANTINE AND PETER GLASSGOLD

MARSILIO PUBLISHERS
NEW YORK

Original bilingual German/Italian edition:
Gegenstände/Oggetti
Published All'Insegna del Pesce D'Oro
Copyright © 1995 Hans Deichmann and Vanni Scheiwiller

Translation copyright © 1997 Marsilio Publishers

Of the present edition © 1997
Marsilio Publishers
853 Broadway, Suite 600
New York, New York 10003 USA

ISBN 1-568860-48-X

WHY? HOW COME?
(A technical preface)

"You should write down all the things you've been telling me all these years about your life," a woman friend told the chronicler, H.D., in 1974. Obediently, he wrote a number of inconclusive letters—then the project ground to a halt.

Fourteen years later, a new friend urged him: "You are one of the people who lived through those terrible German years, and one of the few who took account what was actually going on. You must write down what happened, otherwise priceless knowledge will be irretrievably lost to future generations." But H.D. was strongly against the idea of writing memoirs—as far as he was concerned, that should be left to people like Churchill or Adenauer. He could at most report on events through things he himself had experienced . . . but, for the time being, nothing happened.

In August 1988, H.D. was sitting with a group of friends on a terrace overlooking the Ligurian Sea. One of them was about to leave for an international conference on child psychiatry, and begged H.D. to write an account for her of how he, as an eight-year-old, in an attempt to establish independence from his environment, had spent hours wrapped in vague thoughts, swaying in circles on a swing in the dark. That is how the first "object," "The Spaceship," came to be, along with the decision to give each episode an ordinary object as a title. An object was to be the initial, central, or closing point of each episode, preferably all three.

Thanks to their objectivity, these objects would also help stop the reports from slipping into self-glorifying propaganda for the author. His only wish was to relive with the reader the many disparate events and the moods and feelings attached to them. For this reason, the author decided to follow memories as they came, and forego any chronological ordering noting only the dates on which the reports were drafted. To ensure the necessary, even-handed, objective treatment of all the participants, H.D. appears throughout the book in the third person.

This technique was used successfully in two of the chronicler's previous works: the Italian edition of the letters of H. J. von Moltke, *Futuro e Resistenza—Dalle Lettere degli Anni 1926-1945* (Future and Resistence—From the Letters of 1926-1945), Brescia, 1985; and in the book by and about Dr. Eugenie Schwarzwald, *Leben mit provisorischer Genehmigung* (Living Provisionally), Vienna, 1988.

H.D.'s mother-tongue is German, but having lived in Italy since 1948—half his life—he felt it was important that Ordinary Objects also appear in his adopted language. This led to the original bilingual German/Italian edition. H.D. is grateful to Marsilio Publishers for bringing out the work in English, thereby allowing him to share his life's experiences with a new and wider audience.

·

OBJECTS

A
CHRONICLE
OF
SUBVERSION
IN
NAZI GERMANY
AND
FASCIST ITALY

·

Contents

THE SPACESHIP

Back then, more than seventy years ago, there was as yet no "spaceship" in the vocabulary of science, but as we shall see, She was one, for She moved into unexplored space, cruising under the force of her own mass and the inspiration of her pilot. She was devoted to this first astronaut, to his imagination, needs, and longings.

It was the year before the end of the World War I. The one and only aerial bomb had yet to fall on Cologne, but deservedly, Germany had already begun to lose the war. Those dramatic events had no effect on either the spaceship or the astronaut, for both were still too young and sheltered.

Who was She, and who was He? He was a little fellow, eight years old at most, and She a perfectly ordinary, every-day swing.

When the space travels began, the family had lived scarcely three years in the flight center. This was a palatial, three-story, upper-class house, simple but elegant, on a small square in the old part of town that was shaded by four rows of linden trees and quietly dominated by the house.

One entered the house through a grand entrance-way with a porte-cochère supported by smooth columns. It had been built for horse and carriage, used now for automobiles. On the ground floor facing the square were the cloakrooms and the dining room with three windows and walls, the lower parts of which were wainscotted. These were reached through a quasi-ceremonial, square anteroom, from which a great staircase went up to the second floor, the actual living quarters. The children entered the impressive but comfortable expanse of these rooms with some respect and were tolerated there only on their best behavior. Dirty hands were forbidden. This may have contributed to the beginning of the space travel on the third floor: a little distance gained here, a little there.

Let us linger a bit longer in describing the house. Next to the living room there was a ballroom that in the course of eighteen years rarely saw use. It was richly decorated with frescoes and mirrors on the walls and ceiling and furnished with gilt chairs and deep, rose-colored silk sofas—under protective throw covers, of course. During the First World War, the children were allowed to construct their model railroad there. When a fire broke out on the railroad bridge, not only was the train engulfed in flames, but the parquet floor was damaged in the catastrophe as well—a fact that was only discovered by the lady of the house after the war. It also happened one day that the roofers informed her that four roof-ridges were missing their anchoring lead plates. A puzzle to be sorted-out . . . She told this to her sons, who were now students, at dinner one evening and was met with gales of laughter: "We used the plates to cast lead soldiers!" During the war, in that unheated ballroom, there were three railroaders: H.D., his brother, and their closest friend of the same age, the son of the chauffeur. Together they ran a railway with over ten meters of track and were dressed for winter, with kneepads to save their precious stockings from irrevocable destruction through sliding around on the floor.

On the ground floor looking out onto the courtyard were the large kitchen and storerooms, the servants' dining room, the pantry with its enormous cupboards for cutlery and dishes, and another small room used only for cleaning silver and shoes. This part of the house, reserved for the servants, lay a few steps below street level, leaving space for a small, low, intermediate story that had bedrooms for two valets and the servants' bath. When the bathroom window was open, the little scions of the house, standing below in the courtyard, could raise up the bath curtain with a long stick and so provoke a frightful scolding from Minna in the tub. Minna—who based her demand for respect on the fact that she had lived in the house longer than the astronaut—didn't realize that the disrespectful boys were obliged to stand directly under the window in order to hold up the curtain and couldn't even see her head over the edge of the tub.

Back stairs went up from the kitchen area, and even the masters of the house had to use them to get from the second floor to the third, space-travel floor, which is why that stretch of stairway was provided with a carpet runner. Before H.D. and his dear readers climb all the way to the top, let us call to mind one more significant place on the second floor: the toilet! The modernizers of the old house had run into difficulties in their efforts to create sufficient facilities, which they overcame by installing a toilet on each landing of the back stairs. The one on the second floor had for the younger denizens of the house a luxury all its own: a window at sitting height. One could sit and do one's business while talking to playmates in the courtyard, arguing with them, badgering them, insulting them: "I won't! Leave my bike alone!" "Are you blind? The ball's stuck in the ivy behind the Venus!" (This was a cast-iron Venus of Cyrene given to H.D.'s great-grandfather by old Alfred Krupp. The boys loved her beautiful womanly body, because by putting one foot on a breast and the other on a shoulder, one could reach the top of the wall of the neighboring house.)

Having reached the third floor, H.D. begs to pause once more. The memory of the five children's rooms, with their view over the tops of the linden trees to St. George's church across the square still warms his heart after seventy years. The two boys and their sister, three years younger, each had a room, and there was one for their nanny. In the middle was a big playroom with two windows. Their parents slept on the courtyard side. All the rooms were connected to each other and to the landing by doors, crucial for the wonderful game they played, which any grownup who happened to be around would join with zeal: hide-and-seek. The whole floor was darkened. Then began the running and hiding in stocking-feet. Sneaking up and seizing those who were hidden was more important than running, though naturally if you were being hunted, you ran, because you were "it" only if you were touched and named at the same time.

The landing was a large passageway, approximately 5x8 meters, separated from the back stairs by a door. The only illumination came through a skylight. It was there that a cross-bar had been installed with a pair of sturdy rings to hold a swing. This led a double life. Sometimes that of an ordinary swing, able to ride far out—which it did frequently and gladly—because of the size and height of the area. At other times, suitably metamorphosed, touched in the depths of its inmost being, it became a spaceship. It was launched fairly high from the floor and, during its journey to the unknown, tried to avoid colliding with the large toy-filled wardrobe on the left of the door to the stairs, and on the opposite wall, with a large chest—the very one, incidentally, that allowed the little astronaut to board his ship and sit astride it—facing the wardrobe. Rocket engine and pilot in one, he pulled the two lengths of rope on one side of the swing toward himself and then pushed them away bending his body slightly to the right, then to the left. This made the swing—now a true spaceship in the cosmos—take on a circular motion.

The two circled seemingly endlessly, in fact often hours at a time. Usually this happened toward evening in the fading light or even in complete darkness. The astronaut took his bearings, the time, and the course from the skylight, at which he often threw inquiring glances. The slowly increasing darkness was occasionally interrupted by light from the ironing room in the attic, whose windows opened onto the shaft of the skylight. He accepted this—he had no choice—but didn't care for it at all, since it interrupted his cruising through the separate world that was his one and only concern. This world was barely felt, without definite substance, but it was precisely this peculiar quality that gave him protection against everything else going on around him: he did not have to take a position on things, and it put him beyond the many categories of life that scared him. Circling and swaying, he remained alone with himself and his unspoken longings. It also happened that he murmured to himself, rhythmically repeating apparently senseless words. H.D. recalls one of those half-articulated mouthings: "The return is much nicer, much nicer . . ."—apparently the return to a different place of safety open to him alone.

In the late afternoon, his mother usually came up to look in on the children's rooms. When she entered the landing through the door next to the wardrobe and saw the space travel in progress, she didn't turn on the light, but feeling her way across to the playroom, carefully avoided the circling ship and let the astronaut know by gestures or a few reassuring words that he should go ahead. At that hour, however, this meant only a short reprieve. In the end, the needs of the other residents of the house forced the spaceship to stop . . . until the next voyage.

The yearning for similar flights into space—satisfied from time to time, but never in its original, consummate form—has stayed with H.D. to this day.

July 1988

A LARGE CURTAIN OF YELLOW SILK

What's so important about a yellow curtain? the reader may ask. Where did it hang and for what purpose? Was it of more use than curtains normally are? Apparently so, for how else would it have gained the status of a chapter title? Like the rest of its kind, it protected a window—in this case a particularly large one—from prying eyes. In short, it concerned itself with discretion, a practice which comes easily only to curtains. But to learn how seriously our curtain took its task, we must ask the reader to be patient.

On a cosy little square in the oldest part of Cologne, a venerable but lively city, stood a patrician house (modernized, however, in 1913) of staid and modest elegance. The entrance-way led to a ceremonial reception hall on the first floor, unpretentious in both its size and in its furnishings. There five possible paths converged. Dominating them all was a free-standing staircase to the second floor, in addition to four doors that led to various entrances and exits. The largest of them, almost as imposing as the staircase, was a double door opening on to the smooth bright columns resting on black marble pedestals and supporting the roof of the porte-cochère. You would probably call it a glass door if its many small polished panes were not framed in such broad, irregular bronze grillwork that it was scarcely possible to see into the reception hall. Fascinated as they were by the beauty of this doorway, people nevertheless found it uninviting, and visitors, entering the house from the street via the porte-cochère were guided by their knowledge of local custom, or by a servant, to approach the actual interior of the house through the cloakrooms to the left. Only now did one reach the reception hall, through the second door on the front side of the room opposite the staircase. On the same side, the third door opened on to the spacious dining room, or rather dining hall, with its three windows facing the street. We will enter it later, in company with the invited guests. The much smaller fourth door, on the right next to the staircase, was used only by those who knew of it, because it was screened by the very strong, blinding light that streamed across from the staircase. It connected the reception hall with the back rooms, which were on a slightly lower level, where the household staff went about its duties.

We are concerned primarily with the great staircase. Its window, the source of the aforementioned flood of light, was hidden in the evening by a yellow-silk curtain. Here lies the scene of the crime in our narrative but some patience will be required before a full testimony on the deed can be provided.

The staircase had two flights diverging one from the other, the first from the reception hall up to a broad rectangular landing and the other up from there to the residence on the third floor. About a man's height above the landing, there was a kind of balcony with flowerboxes instead of a balustrade and with a window seat on which an enormous window rested. We shall see the importance of this later. Coming up from below, you saw the sky—in memory always blue—and after conquering the first steps, there appeared in the window frame the crown of a mighty chestnut tree, still alive today, and so big that all by itself it turned the courtyard into a garden.

The staircase not only served the family in its everyday routine of climbing to the living quarters and descending to the noon and evening meals, but also served guests, who were always received on the second floor. Receptions, then known as *dîners*—and not to be confused with the informal "Cocktail-parties" that came into being much later—were meticulously prepared evening meals, testimony to the traditional and secure status of the hosts and their high level of culture. First on the agenda for these dinners was a well thought-out roster of guests: powerful men in business, either of the same class as the hosts or on the rise; important figures in the municipal government; high-ranking bureaucrats (in the Rhineland more accepted than respected); representatives of the musical life of the city and other intellectuals who, in concert with the hostess, seemed suitable as a hedge against banality or even boredom; and sometimes, too, "well-bred" members of the extended family.

Just as important for the inevitable success of the dinners was the deliberate seating plan. Everything had to be right hierarchically, politically, and erotically: an elegant menu borrowed from the French; the flower arrangements on the table; and sometimes little details intended to highlight the exceptional nature of the evening. In the preparations just as in the actual course of the evening, the hostess was the unquestioned center of activity at these "court receptions," and the object of deserved deference. Most of the necessary requirements for such events were to be found in the self-sufficient household, but these dinners also required outside help in the form of a specialized chef; a trusted florist responsible for the table arrangements, which evidenced painstaking care and imagination; additional servants; and the chauffeur transformed into a doorkeeper.

In order to savor the approaching action, a digression concerning the general atmosphere of the house will be useful. It was a happy mixture of mutual benevolent respect, trust, and lasting friendship over the years, more solidarity than hierarchy. All participants respected the roles of the others and played their own with diligence. The people who were asked to help in the household were trusted. Before they had become doormen or office assistants in the bank of the lord of the house, they—here H.D.'s pen balks at the word "servants"—had been employed by one branch or another of the family as household help. They had been a part of the establishment longer than the children and were therefore regarded by them as older friends, by whose knowledge or under whose protection things were allowed that were otherwise frowned upon. An example. H.D., by now around fifteen, met Heinrich—who had become a bank messenger—not far from the entrance to his father's bank. Heinrich was laughing so hard he did not notice H.D. and so could not throw him the usual familiar words of greeting. H.D. rushed into the porter's lodge and stormily demanded to hear the joke that had just been told there. He was told that a dockworker had fallen into the Rhine. He couldn't swim, as was common in those days, so his workmates quickly threw him a rope. When they finally hauled him out, they asked him what he had been thinking of in the water. He answered, "I was thinking, if I let go the line, them three'd fall flat on their asses!" Other such anecdotes, mostly "clean," characteristic of Cologne and its inhabitants, were picked up from these friends by the scions of the house.

Back to the dinner. The children took an active part in the preparations, running around everywhere. In the kitchen, they looked into the pots. In the dining room, they followed with excitement the creation of the flower arrangements on the table. They gazed in wonder at the Wedgwood tableware that was brought out for such occasions, with the gold-rimmed plates monogrammed "C.T.D.," as well as their great-grand-mother's gold dessert forks. (There were thirteen of these, so they could only be used for the smaller dinners. The thirteenth was originally intended to replace one that had been mislaid, but which turned up again many years later when a ball gown of the great-grandmother's was ripped up. How many poor housemaids had been suspected of the theft?) Finally, they studied the seating plan posted in the reception hall. They recognized many of the names. The number of guests—expected at 8 p.m.—varied between ten and twenty. Since they generally arrived punctually, one had to take up one's post in good time.

Where then was the scene of the crime? On the window seat behind the large, yellow-silk curtain. There they positioned themselves, the pair of them, the two brothers, and eventually the three of them, when they reluctantly allowed their sister, who was three years younger, to join them. The smallest move-ment would have led without fail, and with incalculable conse-quences, to the discovery of the observation post. But, thank goodness, such a catastrophe never happened.

Behind the yellow curtain, the watchers waited in antic-ipation. The unsuspecting guests stepped out of the cloak-room into the entrance hall and scrutinized the seating arrangements, which were posted on the large table between the doors described previously and pointed out by the butler in his black tailcoat. One could see how they withheld their comments on account of the butler. With every step of the stairs, they came closer to the eyes behind the tiny slits in the curtain and became more talkative, whispering to one another. Unfor-tunately for the watchers their talk was seldom discernible.

They were mostly couples, and it was fiendishly hard for the spies to suppress their giggles, since now the expected thing usually happened: the ladies, worried about their décolletage, suddenly gave their brassieres a final tug, or pulled their garter belts straight, or smoothed their hips because the extremely short, practically mini, sack dresses then fashionable should not show a waist. The younger of the two watchers followed this particular motion with an expertise he had gained from accompanying his mother to the seamstress, where—to the customer's loss—his opinion was not always heeded. The men usually checked with a pat of their hands that their hair and mustaches were neat and their bowties and dinner jackets straight. Frequently, too, they checked their trousers' most precious contents which was customarily dressed to the left (the right side being given over to their wallets). After the unavoidable turn of the stairs, the guests could not help but show their backs to the eyes of the watchers, in whose unsparing judgment girth, apparel, and the swaying of the lower half of the body played a decisive role. When they reached the top, the guests, now wholly concerned with dignity, disappeared from the watchers view.

The pleasurable observation of these individuals was crowned by their procession down the stairs, after the butler hurried in to announce to the lady of the house: "Dinner is served, Madam!" The guests meanwhile had greeted each other on the upper floor, and the gentlemen joined the ladies who were to be their dinner companions. The "single" male guests brought up the rear. In this formation, led by the hostess, they proceeded down to the dining hall. Their mother knew about the watchers, and even if there was no motion in the curtain to confirm their presence, she looked up at it and winked, with a little smile, despite the possibility that her dinner companion might think that the smile was directed at him.

By now the young legs were stiff after more than a half-hour of standing stockstill, and so the watchers happily abandoned the hospitable window seat and the protective yellow curtain, highly pleased with their pickings. But that was not enough. They mingled with those who worked behind the scenes, going through the kitchen to the serving pantry, a few steps higher than the kitchen, separating it from the dining hall. From there, through a crack in the door, they could admire the table and, in the middle, their regal mother.

It is worth noting that no one ever said a word to the watchers about approving these so-called dinners as proper models for a social style that would end soon afterward, much less considering them worth striving for and emulating. Those concerned noticed the end only when their financial positions forced them to. Those hidden behind the curtain were simply amusing themselves in their own way, and that was all. The dinners did not even figure as examples of life in "the old days" but remained a curiosity about which H.D. tells what he thinks is a good story, hoping that his readers find it so too. The chronicler has been unable to find a conclusive date for this narrative. His parents sent him to boarding school in 1923, and by then, almost sixteen, he would have been too old to play the watcher anyway. It might possibly have been the year before, but 1922 was the worst year of inflation after World War I. Did the privileged classes already have so much money again and so little conscience to allow such festivities? At the end of 1923 came the stabilized mark and with it the start of the economic boom . . . and behind the yellow curtain, the chronicler's sister stood alone.

September 1988

The Chamber Pot of Santa Chiara

When, where, and how did this chamber pot share the fate allotted to its kind? The chronicler, H.D., can easily provide the answer, but to do so he must start at the very beginning, confident of his reader's subsequent approbation.

Many people may still recall that in 1939 to the applause of the German people, a *Gastarbeiter* (immigrant worker) from Austria named Hitler, Adolf began a war of aggression that by May 1945 ended badly for all concerned, especially for the *Gastarbeiter*'s adopted *Volk und Reich* ("People and Empire"). The Germans wanted to forget the war and the crimes of Hitler and his henchmen as quickly as possible. Only his friend Stalin (in August 1939, they had promised never to harm each other) behaved almost the same. So the Germans threw themselves zealously into clearing away the ruins they themselves had brought about, and today, Mr. Kohl's Kale is flourishing so well that people now find it hard even to imagine the bygone days. [Editor's note: Here and below H.D. is relying on the scatological sense of *Kohl* in German as formally, "kale" or cabbage—whence presumably flatus—, and colloquially, "rubbish."]

We aren't really supposed to rehash the past anymore, but our chamber pot has good grounds to disagree, being older than Mr. Kohl and not given to lying as much as Mr.

Waldheim. Also, as we shall see, it played an active part in clearing away the ruins. But we can comfort Ernst Nolte and his ilk (German historians who would put the past behind us, forever) with the assurance that the previous users of the chamber pot are gone forever. Furthermore the pot itself and its contents seem to have mysteriously disappeared.

Germany lay almost completely in ruins. What the enemy had left standing, the Germans destroyed all by themselves. The few who resisted this eleventh-hour madness were murdered by the Nazis, which like most of their other crimes went unpunished. Please note, moreover, that the chamber pot was Italian-made and had nothing to do with Germany's material ruin, but rather its moral devastation, whose extent was certainly more thorough.

H.D. returned home to the vicinity of Frankfurt at the beginning of September 1945. Like most returnees, he was unemployed, but also full of expectant enthusiasm for participating in the spiritual reconstruction, the attempt to remove the foundations and habits of fascism—from the right and from the left—which were so ingrained in the Germans. There were only a few people with whom he could associate, for only a few had had the strength and the good fortune to keep themselves at an uncompromising distance from National Socialism. In Frankfurt, some of these people were connected to academe. The obvious step was to reopen the universities as quickly as possible. Easy to say, harder to do. That didn't simply mean windows in empty window frames and, in place of the even emptier Nazi professors, teachers with integrity. The crucial thing was to demand something *new* in place of the old order, which even before 1933 had been unable to prevent the moral collapse.

In 1927, nine years after the end of the first German war of aggression, Kafka's great friend Milena Jesenska wrote in a report on the International Werkbund Exhibition of architecture and design in Stuttgart: "... One wonders why Germany, which is so full of extraordinary talents, a country with a sense of order and discipline, is so terribly gray and so sad, despite all the praise it has earned. There is probably no other country with such an absolute separation between the intellectual elite and the rest of the people. ... only in Germany can a Goethe and a Mozart have nothing to say to the man in the street."

H.D., an "ordinary," "uneducated" man for whom feeling that he was a member—nothing more!—of the intellectual elite was always made difficult, was all too familiar with this typically German rule of the game. He and his friends understood their mission in 1945. They had to cooperate with anything that might be appropriate, not so much in erasing the arbitrary boundaries between the intellectual and the practical spheres of activity, but in getting all the participants to see something normal and indispensable in fruitful exchange. Down with *l'art pour l'art*!

As a first step toward the revitalization of the university, the Forum Academicum was opened in Frankfurt, in November 1945, for the purpose of arranging evening lectures and discussions. The first report, in March 1946, declares:

"The Americans make a very precise distinction between 'education,' that is, training and instruction (especially of the young), and 'information,' the instruction and informing of adults (which ought to continue throughout their entire lives). Significantly, German has no proper translation for 'information.' Germans have always been very well 'educated'— apart from the last twelve Nazi years—that is to say, well taught in school, but as adults they have been poorly 'informed' about matters that move mankind and encouraged even less to think for themselves.

"The Forum Academicum will endeavor to provide 'information' to the broadest possible public, by allowing world problems and events to be presented and inviting members of the public to offer up their own opinions in the discussion.

"If in so doing the Forum Academicum relies on the universities . . . it is also to bring about in Germany the contact between the university and the public at large, which is traditional in Anglo-Saxon countries. . . ."

Willy Hartner and Hans Deichmann, the two people responsible, can thank the Cultural Section of the Military Government, that this undertaking was able to be put in motion with incredible speed. Already on December 6, 1945, Professor Georg Hohmann spoke on the topic, "Do Spiritual Possibilities Exist for Us?" The American friends of the I.C.D. (Information Control Division) in Bad Homburg took care of everything: gas and tires for two small cars brought out from hiding; enormous quantities of gray cardboard with which the windows of the Great Hall of the University were "weatherproofed;" and chalk for the large blackboard behind the podium. But even the Americans could not conjure up heating. They did, however, furnish electric lighting for the Great Hall and for the damaged stairway to the second floor. Despite these less than inviting outward conditions, public attendance was beyond all expectations. For the ten events in the winter of 1945-46, four to six hundred freezing people were present, so great was the desire to clear away the moral wreckage and the wish to share in the creation of something new. The results of this undertaking and its quiet demise in the summer of 1948 would merit a separate report. But we must not lose sight of the chamber pot in Rome. (And with this, we have revealed its whereabouts.)

The efforts to revive the universities in the American

occupied zone continued. For this reason, representatives of the universities convened in Marburg in the summer of 1946 for an exchange of ideas and experiences. If he remembers correctly, H.D. took part as the only unaffiliated, ordinary man. The lapse into the old demarcations had already begun.

Also participating at Marburg was Ernesto Grassi, an Italian professor of philosophy who had held a teaching position in Munich during the National Socialist period. He was certainly no Fascist, but like most Italians with whom H.D. had come in contact in the years 1942-45, he was a master of disguise. Now he came from Rome with a commission to invite a few German professors guaranteed not to be Nazis and, if possible, with reputations abroad, to attend the International Congress of Philosophy planned for late November 1946. Grassi's choice fell on Julius Ebbinghaus (by then rector at Marburg), Walter Hallstein (rector at Frankfurt), Willy Hartner (professor at Frankfurt), and H.D.

"But I'm not a philosopher," said H.D., "much less a professor. How did you think of me?"

"Not important. Without you, the other three will never get to Rome."

Grassi was a true clairvoyant. Events proved he was completely right. H.D. had his hands full over the next four months clearing away seemingly insurmountable obstacles. There were exit permits from the American zone to be procured, German passports, Italian visas, permits to travel through the French zone and through Switzerland, tickets (or what substituted for them in those days), the smallest amount of pocket money possible for the journey (the visitors would be in Rome as guests), and so on.

At last the journey began. These were the first German participants in an international congress since the end of the war! It was something so extraordinary that the mayor of Frankfurt put his car at their disposal to take them to the railway station at Karlsruhe, the nearest place from which trains to Switzerland departed. In Karlsruhe, the travelers spent the night in the station's air-raid shelter, now a hotel, two levels underground, in stalls open at the top like toilets and furnished with plank beds.

Early the next morning, the journey continued on a train for American soldiers on furlough, thanks of course to a special permit. The train stopped at Singen, the border station with Switzerland. Suddenly, the command was given, "All civilians off!" Surprised, the four perplexed travelers found themselves on the platform with their baggage. It was not so easy after all to reach the rubble-free world. Then, Fortune twice provided consolation. The first was in the shape of an ill-clothed and malnourished woman who offered, for a small fee, to escort them and take their baggage in a small handcart as far as the border, a journey that would take twenty minutes. Then, after they had stowed their baggage on the cart, a well-nourished, well-dressed fellow—he could only be an American—came up to them and asked almost shyly if there might be room on the cart for his small suitcase. Here was the second consolation. Everyone knew English, so a lively conversation ensued. Yes, he said, he was an American, a diplomat, but a civilian, and like the four travelers had had to leave the military train before the border. After they crossed the frontier on foot and were standing on Swiss soil, with the four helpless Germans on the lookout for transportation, the American offered to take them in his taxi—an enormous Cadillac—to the station at Basel.

They accepted with pleasure, but not the invitation to lunch, since they already had another appointment. This had to do with the Swiss francs that H.D.'s brother had deposited at a coal merchant's near the railway station. They had not seen a street so clean in years. The doorknobs of the houses, polished to a shine, seemed like treasures from an enchanted world. "Excuse me, Herr Ebbinghaus, but I don't think you should be doing that right now." He was just about to bend down and pick up the butts of some very long cigarettes that were only two-thirds smoked, in order to roll new ones from them, as he was accustomed to do at home. Cheerful at being free from habitual deprivations, and intoxicated by a forgotten normality, they reached the coal merchant's. At the cashier's booth, H.D. gave his name shyly but hopefully. The petite young lady smiled reassuringly, pulled open a drawer under the counter, and took out two 500-franc notes. The four travelers stood gaping. Trembling, H.D. wrote his name on the receipt, and they left the coal merchant's in anxious silence. Once outside, they looked at each other incredulously. "I was expecting a hundred, or two hundred francs at most . . . So now let's eat!" A huge veal roast garnished with peas, carrots, and green beans did the trick.

The four now went their separate ways for two days, so they could go about their personal business. H.D. only needed to take telephone messages and see to the train tickets. When he arrived at their rendezvous in the station restaurant, Ebbinghaus waved to him from afar with gestures of despair. "You're here at last! I've just smoked a cigar and can't pay for it!" The damage was quickly repaired, and H.D. provided each of them with enough money for cigars.

The last shared adventure in this enchanted world was the trip to the bathroom. There, for a fee of ten centimes, you could withdraw into a stall reminiscent of the Karlsruhe hotel. The receipt dated November '46, testimony to H.D.'s intoxication with such cleanliness, has been preserved ever since in his archives.

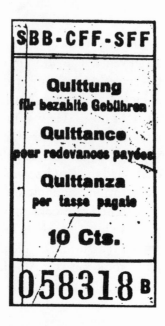

Two days later, they met again at the railway station in Lucerne for their journey on to Rome.

No one should forget that up to that point, 1946 had already been a very eventful year. In January, Austria's pre-Nazi boundaries were recognized. In the spring, the first local elections were held in the Western zones (later the Federal Republic of Germany)—much too early, in the opinion of H.D. and his friends. In the Soviet zone, there had been since April 21st the single Socialist Unity Party, acting as a preliminary to the German Democratic Republic. On April 2nd, Italy decided on a republic. And on May 15th, the Cold War began, in consequence of the failed Peace Conference in Paris.

The Congress of Philosophy was held in Rome at the Palazzo Madama, in the Senate building, where H.D. and the others were to register. Their reception was friendly but reserved, so that the four were not surprised when Professor Grassi, who had issued the invitation in Marburg, took them aside. He told them that not everyone was in agreement with the Germans' participation—some people had protested publicly against it—and so he urged them to be extremely discreet. Like good little schoolboys, they promised their best behavior. It had been obvious to them in advance that "the Germans" represented a burden for the organizers that was not to be underestimated. However, already by the second day, during the work of the various committees, everything seemed to have settled down, with little sign of a special reserve toward the Germans. In fact, Professor Ebbinghaus was asked to assume the chairmanship of one of the committees, because the colleague originally appointed, a Frenchman, was never on time!

The four stayed at the Santa Chiara, a small and very old hotel behind the Pantheon and close by Piazza Minerva. Professor Ebbinghaus wanted at all costs to live up to the German reputation for punctuality and asked H.D. to wake him at a predetermined hour. They slept in high beds with iron frames—very good beds, by the way—but there were no toilets . . . and so in the morning, Ebbinghaus's chamber pot, not unused, protruded from under his bed. It was a splendid pot, ample and old, probably enameled, and suited the furniture, but this did not prevent H.D. from reproaching himself for his lack of discretion. One doesn't go looking into the chamber pots of German philosophers, nor does one allow oneself to find the sight unpleasant. However, duty before all, said H.D. to himself. And so it came to pass that the chamber pot of Santa Chiara, thanks to the continual replaying of its destiny and its devotion to its appointed purpose, has remained in the forefront of his recollections of his first post-Nazi contact with the outer world. The chronicler begs forgiveness.

None the worse for the experience, H.D. took part in the congress with a strong and primarily political interest focused on the plenary sessions. He used the remaining time to meet up with his many friends and acquaintances from the days of March 1942 to December 1943, when he had served as an official representative in Rome of the National Socialist Ministry of Armaments. The exchange of reminiscences about successful rescue and sabotage actions as well as the reassurance that no one would any longer be misunderstood were by turns moving and consoling. Furthermore, one mustn't forget the satisfaction—shared here—of having kept evil within bounds. Our mutual gratitude was enthusiastically revived.

On the third day came the announcement: "Tomorrow evening, Pope Pius XII will receive the congress." High enthusiasm everywhere! "But," objected the three Protestant German professors, "we will not kneel before the pope." H.D.'s argument, that for nonbelievers kneeling before the pope was only a gesture of politeness, fell on deaf ears. (It had been more out of sport than for moral scruples that H.D. had always avoided swearing allegiance to Hitler.) H.D.'s distress that three distinguished German professors in the autumn of 1946 (one and half years after Hitler) felt such a dilemma worthy of consideration went entirely unnoticed . . . because after careful reflection, he left it unexpressed.

The audience was held in one of the halls at the Vatican. Some two hundred seated philosophers waited for the pope for a good half-hour. When he appeared, they *all* rose. And they all knelt when the pope invited them to pray together . . . except for H.D. He was so intent at observing how his professors comported themselves that he forgot about kneeling himself. What a sight! The three of them lying there, like felled trees. And smiling with pleasure at this, H.D. too, knelt down.

October 1988

HAYRACKS

The chronicler, H.D., is firmly resolved that every story of his worth telling must have an ordinary *object* as its starting point, central point, or conclusion. This obliges him invite "The Rack" to jump in and take the place in the title of some living creatures, "The Vinegar Factory Horses."

No need for panic. It is well known that hayracks do not jump, but also that horses are not supposed to rake. But to each horse his own rack. The doubt of know-it-alls concerning the authenticity of the word *Raufe* ("hayrack") was overcome at a stroke by Duden's great, multivolume *Dictionary of Origins* where we find (p. 553), under the verb *raufen*, right at the end: "hayrack [*Raufe*] a manger from which livestock rake [*rupft*] the fodder (Late Middle High German '*roufe*')." Let the reader disregard the fact that human beings also rake at one another when they raise a ruckus; that the politician's moneybag of choice for holding raked-off taxes is known as a rack; and finally, that H.D. cannot bring himself to put the highly aristocratic horse in the same "livestock" category as the politician. So let us stay with mangers for horses, and let us get to the point, but with no fear of diversions.

The family house in Cologne was located in the Old City on the long eastern side of the small comfortable square already known to the reader. On its southern side were two other buildings that played a role in the children's lives during and immediately after World War I whose importance should not be underestimated. The first, a dilapidated house bordering an old square and a row of nondescript sheds, filled out the corner of the square. Here were kept the horse, wagon, and a not very large store of charcoal briquettes belonging to a *Klüttebor* by the name of Enders. (A *Klüttebor* was what one called a street-peddler who sold by the kilo neatly stacked, small charcoal bricks, *Klütten*, from a flat, one-horse cart fitted with heavy scales.) Herr Enders went by the family house several times a day. H.D. thinks he can hear the clatter of the hoofs and the metal-rimmed wheels on the bumpy pavement and greetings and chitchat in Kölsch, the local dialect. And so it came to pass in 1921, when the former Empress Augusta left this world in Holland, and H.D.'s father had the old black, white, and red flag flown from the balcony at half-mast despite the protests of the entire family, Enders asked, "You're in mourning for your flagpole?" This question, so politically apt, entered into the family vocabulary, where it did excellent duty in the confusions of the postwar years.

At noon, the official car of the mayor of Cologne drove into the courtyard. H.D.'s parents, without a car because of the war, had lent out their chauffeur. In the solemn black automobile with its dark red upholstery and faded pink-gray curtains, lowered for the occasion, H.D. was graphically initiated into the first mysteries of male equipment by Hermann, the chauffeur's son, who was one year older than H.D. and the inseparable playmate of him and his brother.

But that was much later. For many years, what was of unrivaled importance to the children was the second building bordering the courtyard, a well-kept but barely used two-story tanner's warehouse whose long entranceway led to a spacious garden full of old trees with tall trunks, bushes, wild-flowers, and stretches of unkempt lawn. This little park actually belonged to a nearby apartment house, which ignored it. The building's front entrance was on another street and seemed a long way off to the children.

H.D. and his brother and sister had a key to this oasis in the big city and permission to enter with their playmates at any time. The actual owners of the garden were never in sight, but there was a kind of line of demarcation that the children respected, in order not to be bothered in turn. Almost every day, they sought out this special arena—both spacious and hidden—for their games. One could also go there alone and make believe he was safe from the rest of the world with its countless threats, against which there was no possibility of defense.

On the side opposite the entranceway, the garden was bounded by a brick wall, four or five meters high and black with age. To climb it, one had to support oneself by scrambling with one leg in the knotholes of a nearby tree and the other braced against the wall, in a space forty centimeters wide at best. At the top, one crawled over a corrugated-iron roof a few meters wide to a row of narrow windows that admitted dim light into the stable on the ground floor of the warehouse of a vinegar factory. The occupants of the stable, three or four in number, usually returned in the late afternoon from their labors in the streets of Cologne, stretched out their four legs while standing, and gave themselves up to eagerly raking from their racks. Considering that for the horses this was the most important event of the day, even a historian must admit that the choice of title for this account is not misleading, especially since the crime that now follows depends on the rack. Exactly who it was that hatched the mischief is gone from memory. (Ernst Nolte will be content.) It was probably not the chronicler, who loved animals very much and had inherited from his father a passion for horses. Nevertheless, he joined so enthusiastically in the execution of the deed that he must be included here in the national pastime of overcoming the past.

In short, the three ten-year-old boys used to band together to fling pebbles through the windows at the weary horses, otherwise peacefully occupied with raking the fodder from their racks. This was not a deliberate tormenting of the animals so much as a desire for an enjoyable effect: extreme unrest in the stable, snorting, angry neighing, and even bucking. One might suppose the horses were fighting with each other. Then the stableboy would appear, and so on top of everything else, the poor horses were yelled at and urged to calm down. This would not last long. As soon as the tormentors believed themselves safe again, they would loose a second rain of pebbles on the horses' backs. The same result, except that one time it was not the stableboy who came, but a uniformed lieutenant—so it must have been 1917 or the spring of 1918. He charged into the stable, cursing loudly, and immediately spotted the throwers at the windows. He dashed into the courtyard while shouting his furious threats, seized a ladder, and made unmistakable preparations to climb up to the corrugated-iron roof and punish the malicious brats. But knowing what was coming, they sat down with their legs dangling from the edge of the high black wall. The menacing avenger in uniform approached them, stepping gingerly. The roof did not support him as safely as it did the lighter criminals, who knew the spot. Then, they jumped down into the garden one after another, where the soft earth, as they knew from experience, offered them a gentle reception. Above stood the astonished lieutenant, helpless and not knowing whether to shout further threats or admire the daredevil jumpers.

After that, the horses were no longer pestered. H.D. and his accomplices, however, were certain to find other subjects for their cruel pleasures.

March 1989

DUTCHMEN

The people strolling along the Rhine Promenade in Cologne scattered between the Hohenzollern Bridge and the restaurant called Bastei, an ancient redoubt on the river. Some were amused, some indignant. Others laughed or made threats, were surprised or scolding. A few even admired the drivers' skill. In any case, that is how the chronicler, H.D., remembers the way it was, seventy-five years ago, sitting at the extreme back of the vehicle.

Friends now accuse H.D. of hiding behind the grammatical third person. He esteems the ladies who reproach him far too much for him not to proceed this once for their sakes with "I" and "we." That comes easy to him, because the actors here are few in number.

"What is really going on?" those readers will ask who are always inclined to be impatient. It is advisable to keep them in good spirits and not cast their impatience to the winds. It happened by the Rhine, but how and where? What kind of vehicle, suited to rob pedestrians of their meditations? Who were the drivers, and how many were they? Could the vehicle have caused traffic problems like those of today, which no one can control? Did it perhaps emit a toxic exhaust? (No, not toxic.)

In trying to answer these questions, I (H.D.) came up

against a primary, you might say existential, difficulty. I had to describe the vehicle, its form and its soul, and in so doing give some insight into the hearts of the drivers, the guardians of that soul. A visual representation was indispensable. After attempting some clumsy and worthless sketches, I got the helpful idea of asking the Nuremburg Toy Museum for assistance. And lo, a miracle occurred, but of the kind you can truly rely on. The hoped-for deliverance was forthcoming, following an exchange of letters with the directress, the mainstay of the institute, who made me wish the story of the Dutchmen would never come to an end.

The illustration from the Nuremburg Archive—part of a Dutch advertisement from the first years of our century—shows a small, two-seat vehicle that boasts the name Flying Dutchman, for which its primitive power transmission (arm propulsion) disqualifies it. Our own—mine and those of my brother Carl and our friend Hermann—were one-seaters and equipped with gears that helped them reach a speed which panicked the pedestrians. But these vehicles, too, as we shall see, had every reason not to take unto themselves a provocative name. Only Hermann and his Dutchman might have done so in a pinch, if they had not been so occupied in assisting the others of their kind. That giving assistance is satisfying is nothing new—"to do good and do yourself good," as Robert Musil said in tribute to Genia Schwarzwald and her salon—and the same was true here, all the more since Hermann's assistance immediately enhanced the performance of his Dutchman. How was this possible?

The three one-seaters, ridden by their three seven- to eight-year-old drivers, had begun a normal existence in the form in which they were designed, constantly scooting up and down the courtyard of the family house. When it rained, they moved under the cover of the spacious porte-cochère, where driving on the white, grooved flagstones produced a mighty din, music for those who caused it, but less so for the residents of the house. This leads one to suppose that it wasn't just confidence in the drivers, which increased as we got older, that induced my mother to allow more distant playgrounds for the Dutchmen.

The gate to the street was opened, and the seldom frequented sidewalks round and about Georgsplatz became an expanded track. In order to profit from all the new possibilities, and also to include the asphalt of Georgstrasse, which was not allowed at all in the beginning, you had to make a jump down from the *trottoirs*—as the sidewalks were called in Cologne—and then up again. That is, especially in getting back up, you had to ride against the curbstones at full speed and make the leap onto the *trottoir* easier on the front wheels by lightly shifting your weight backward, like a rider trying to clear a hurdle. But damaging bumps to the front axles could never be completely avoided, so after a while, they began to break. The first breakdown happened to my brother, who was careless with objects. There he stood, with a mechanically perfect Dutchman missing its front axle and wheels. Let it be said to my parents credit that the thought that damaged Dutchmen could be replaced by new ones never entered their minds, not even as a distant consideration. The unhappiness was great, until we discovered that after removing what remained of the front axle, the front wooden fork could be attached with a wire to the rear fork of another Dutchman. Now I was to be left behind on my one-seater when a two-seater was created like the one in the advertisement, but with six wheels and two drive gears. I had already been the youngest of the three, slower and less reckless. But now it was all over for me!

Meanwhile, Follerstrasse and Grosse Witschgasse had been included in the driving territory. The latter was the continuation of Georgstrasse after crossing Follerstrasse, and led down to the Rhine. Of the many narrow streets that led from the Old City to the river, this was the only one which ended just below the level of the quay, so that when it rained heavily, small puddles never failed to form. However, it was not on this account that it was less popular with the Dutchmen, but mainly because driving back up out of the depths was so hard.

Down on the left, just short of the riverbank, An der

Lyskirchen-Gasse connected our Grosse Witschgasse with Filzengraben, a broad and less proletarianized street that also sloped to the Rhine. A girl our own age lived there, with whom we shared the early years of our youth after the period of the Dutchmen. An der Lyskirchen led to a small rise, at whose topmost point our Catholic parish church was situated. Our great-grandmother, in whose house we lived after 1913, must have been a highly respected woman in this part of town. When she went to her reward at over ninety, she or members of the family had provided hard cash to assure that every year, on the anniversary of her death, a Requiem Mass was said for her. My mother, though at the time not yet a Catholic and not religiously inclined, used to attend. She took me along once, when I was certainly no older than eight. On a cold, gloomy November day, we entered the little church, appropriately clad, and sat down in one of the front pews under the sharp glances of the usual old women. In the middle of the Mass, the acolyte, obviously as a messenger from the priest, came over to my mother and whispered something in her ear. My mother, visibly distressed, turned to me and with a quick movement snatched my cap from my head. I wanted to sink for shame into the floor of Romanesque stone. Later, on the way home, my mother laughed about it, but even today I feel how mortified I was.

But we have gotten away from the Dutchmen! Forgive me if I have allowed myself to be carried away by the rich memories associated with the names of the streets. My unhappiness at not being able to follow the two-man Dutchman as it raced ahead, the gap ever increasing, and having to search for my street alone between the legs of the pedestrians and the horses, did not last long, thank God: my front axle also went kaput. This time, there was no hesitation! Immediately, the front of my fork, free of wheels and axle, was fastened with a strong hand to my brother's rear fork. For safety's sake, you had to use heavy-gauge wire. It was the only three-seater Dutchman in Cologne, and with *three* drive gears! You can imagine the concentrated power of this little vehicle. In front at the helm sat our inseparable Hermann, then came Carl, my feared brother (he once answered my mother, who was reprimanding him, that to some of the things I said he could only respond with blows), and finally, me. Even if the two in the forward seats liked to make me feel how submissive I should be, they didn't want to give up the additional pull of my arms or the merriment when we took too tight a curve and, by centrifugal motion, I was forced to exchange my smooth, gripless wooden seat for the asphalt of the street. They stopped right away, gathered me up, slightly damaged . . . and laughed.

With this three-seater, we felt ourselves masters of the street, and essentially we were: all the pedestrians who were bothered or simply amused by the little vehicle that disdained any of the usual games were nevertheless mindful of the safety of these curious children. I cannot stop admiring my mother for permitting the long rides. Perhaps she thought it better to allow what she could not prevent and instead use the opportunity to stir our sense of responsibility.

A frequent goal of our excursions was my grandparents' on the Deutscher Ring, some three or four kilometers from our house. Most of the way was along the Rhine, which was reached by going on Georgstrasse, then left on Follerstrasse, and right again down Filzengraben. By then, the main danger spots were past. The ride continued, always on the *trottoir*. Under the suspension bridge, past the arsenal, leaving the cathedral and the Central Station behind on the left.

Then under the Hohenzollern Bridge to the Bastei, and from there left to the Deutscher Ring. We hit our top speed on the broad Rhine Promenade after the Hohenzollern Bridge.

The vehicle and the always eventful excursions were sources of great satisfaction. In every way, we were something very special. After all, who else in the city of Cologne was on the road in a Dutchman, and a triple one to boot! In their own way, the Dutchmen made us sense what riches there were in living dangerously . . . not to mention the pleasure of catching the smell of the horses under their bellies and in their steaming excrement. Thus the Dutchmen in their time played an unforgettable role in our growing up—thanks to the circumstances and to the people who let us enjoy them to the fullest.

June 1989

Four "Gold" Buttons

Seated at the table in the Osteria del Trentin in Piacenza (where the cuisine, thank God, is Emilian) are two women and two men. One of the women is an architect in Milan. One of the men, H.D., the chronicler, lacks a proper designation of origin. Some call him *il Tedesco* ("the German"), though usually softening it with a friendly and even appreciative smile. But four "gold" buttons will enable him to shed a little light on his origins.

The other woman, the mainstay of the group, runs a studio in Piacenza for handcrafted lithographs, engravings, and etchings. The other man is an antiques dealer and restorer. One often encounters dealers of this kind, but seldom a restorer who is so knowledgably devoted to his profession. The other three are having a deep discussion about the principles involved in a project for converting a church that had been turned over for secular use into a space for exhibitions, concerts, and lectures. H.D. takes advantage of a brief pause in the conversation to ask the restorer about his favorite *objets d'art*. (H.D. always poses such questions when boredom threatens or if there appears to be a favorable opportunity to satisfy his never-ending curiosity.)

Very obligingly, the restorer talks about pictures, furniture, houses, and churches. There is no reaction. But when he mentions with enthusiasm the old horse-drawn coaches and state carriages, something flickers in the chronicler's brain. Suddenly, after seventy-six years four gold buttons bearing the family coat of arms flash before him as if seen with five-year-old eyes (they were made of brass, of course). They had served as decoration on the tails of two livery coats made of silver-beige cloth and were attached at the point where the coats divided for freer leg motion. The livery was worn by a coachman and his assistant, both on the box of a deep-blue coupé with big, bright, yellow rubber-coated wheels that served "Madam," H.D.'s mother, in 1912, for excursions into the city of Cologne. She sometimes took her littlest son along. He does not remember if the coupé was drawn by one or by two horses. But he does remember that it had three windows. There was one in each of the doors, right and left, which could be raised and lowered with dark blue felt straps. The third was a fixed horizontal window at the height of the coach box, where the seated liveried backs blocked any possibility of looking out or of letting in light. The chronicler was also still too small to have tried to look through this window, and so today his inner eye sees only two rigid, headless backs, dignified and lightly jiggling to the rhythm of the hoofbeats. Not that the four buttons excited memories of a series of more or less eventful outings, but rather of small incidents, and the meditations that followed, which have their roots in the house of his birth.

The house at Trankgasse 7a, a double mansion of enormous dimensions built in 1868, was inhabited on one side, toward the Rhine, by H.D.'s immediate family, and on the other by a related branch of the Deichmann clan. It had a two-story, tacked-on "Renaissance-style" façade toward the Domplatz, the cathedral square, and a three-story rear that had no pretensions to style whatsoever. The latter looked out on an old garden with stables from the time of the previous and much more handsome building, which had fallen victim to the square in front of the Central Station. H.D. remembers the darkness of the house that surrounded one as soon as he stepped into the entrance hall and which did not abate until the third floor. There, it was bright. There, all three children had come into the world. And there, their mother had her refuge in the three-windowed breakfast room, where she had her desk and beside it sister Freya's cradle. The three windows are mentioned because through two of them one could look at the façade of the cathedral, while through the other the station square and the Hohenzollern Bridge could be seen. It is reasonable to suspect that this third, much smaller window was put in after the arrival of H.D.'s father's nineteen-year-old bride—the wife of a thirty-nine-year-old man—to help her breathe in that oppressive house. It cannot be seen in the older photographs, but H.D. definitely remembers it.

On March 30, 1911, early in the morning, the two small brothers, aged three and a half and four and a half, were still lying in their cribs, waiting for their nurse. Their father walked into the room, slightly stooped and pulling behind him a little four-wheeled, high-riding wagon. He announced with visible satisfaction that on the previous evening, Carl and Hans had acquired a little sister named Freya, and that it was she who had brought the wagon for them. H.D. does not recall how this momentous news was received. But he does remember how he stared in astonishment and rapture at the little wagon from the white-lacquered crib, half-open at the top (it was no longer completely closed: he was already too old for that). He was also a little bewildered by the surprise of a rare paternal visit at such an early hour. He should be forgiven if at the time he still didn't quite understand what important places the little wagon and the sister would occupy in his life.

The wagon was fitted with four red iron wheels, a box with room at a pinch for four small children, and a handle that could even have served finer folk for yoking a billy goat. But the Deichmanns were not as fine as that. Our handle served only for pulling or for steering downhill, with the help of an outstretched foot of one of the two small occupants of the front seat. This vehicle would have a course of life reminiscent of humans: first sheltered at home, then in a paved courtyard gradually discovering the world, and finally pretending to be a first-class race car, which in this case, too, would end in self-destruction.

Before we launch into this tragic event, it is important (at least for the chronicler) to stay a while longer on the subject of the house at Trankgasse 7a.

H.D.'s flashback in Piacenza had brought back distant memories, but he wanted to check certain facts. He contacted a cousin he had not met before who was up on the family history and asked her if she happened to have any pictures of the pre-1913 house. (1913 was the year it had been torn down.) After all, her grandfather and H.D.'s grandfather had been brothers and had built that house together. His cousin did have pictures, and immediately had some laser-prints made. They definitely helped fill in some of the gaps in his memory, which was limited to the front of the house opposite the cathedral.

A few steps led from the oppressive main door up to the raised ground floor, where a lighter staircase led to the upper floors. Of the ground floor H.D. only remembers two rooms. To the right, facing the cathedral, was the dining room, where the main course for the children was good behavior, strictly monitored by the "Fräulein" and the parents, sitting far away at the head of the table. When fish was served—clean your plate!—H.D. filled his mouth with chewed-up food, and at the first opportunity ran out and spat out everything into the toilet. (Later in life too, he resisted following orders!) The other room, right across from the dining room, was one of the cloak-rooms and served as H.D.'s first schoolroom. In those days, patrician children did not attend public schools for the first couple of years. So H.D. was taught at home for one year, and his brother for two. They loved their tutor very much. He had been the principal of a suburban elementary school and had also been the first tutor of their mother, who had only ever studied with private tutors. As H.D. began learning his ABC's at the grandfatherly tutor's knee, through the French windows he could watch the horses walking "on the longe," that is, they were made to trot in circles, like in a circus, and not have to stand too long in the stables.

From the second floor window the children eagerly watched everything that was going on at the cathedral: processions, the arrival of exalted ecclesiastics, outdoor masses. But the chronicler's only complete memory is of the opening of the Hohenzollern Bridge. The kaiser had come to Cologne for that, and H.D.'s father, as cavalry captain of the Potsdam Ulan regiment, had donned his bright parade uniform of red and blue with gold braid, a black shako on his head. The whole house was filled with excitement, but the high point was the fireworks that evening, and the street lit with countless blue, white, yellow, red, and green lights all the way to the bridge. The train station and the cathedral were also in festive attire. Everything seemed so close as the children looked out of the maternal windows.

In early August 1914, H.D., his brother, and his mother saw his father off to war. He was by now a cavalry captain in field gray. They went to the station, where he got on an ammunition train, made up mostly of open wagons carrying horses, that left at noon for France. H.D. remembers his father and mother standing in the bright sunlight saying goodbye in front of the new office block—the Deichmann Haus—that had just been built on the site of a former block of residential buildings. Although he was already seven years old, H.D. seems to remember hanging on to his mother's skirts. But his shyness left him when his father took him along onto the platform where the horse-filled train was waiting for the commander to arrive. All those horses, three on each side of the wagon, and their grooms sitting on bundles of straw in the center—that was an unforgettable sight. The horses stomped impatiently; they had no idea where they were going . . . the people of that time, even less.

But the reader was promised the tale of "Freya's" little wagon. This is what happened. Usually two of the children sat in the wagon, carefully steering it with their feet as it rolled down the wooded path from the hill on which the Deichmanns, long before the war, had built a comfortable country house. They usually spent the summers there, and during the war there was more food out in the country. The ride down the hill always went well, as the little wagon's capacity to seat four was never tested—until one fateful August day in 1917. The three children and a little girl from the neighborhood, their ages ranging from six to eleven, sat packed so close together that steering was almost impossible. When they reached a big curve at the bottom of the hill, the wagon turned into a race car and began skidding. It capsized, and all the occupants were injured; not badly, but they suffered cuts and bruises all over, which looked like they might take quite a while to heal.

Normally, when something like this happens, mothers bustle about, worrying and fussing. Not in this case! Our mother was furious and ready to punish us if it would have done any good. Her sister Maria was getting married in a couple of days, and we had been selected to be pages for the wedding. Pages covered with cuts and bruises were more than even our liberal mother could deal with. Her wrath left no space for us to mourn for our wrecked little wagon that had fallen by the wayside.

Before we leave the memories conjured by the golden buttons, the chronicler would like to touch on one last minor event. It took place twenty-five years later, at the very spot from which in 1912 his mother's horse-drawn coupé used to leave to drive into town, and proves what fun-loving people the Cologners were even during the Nazi years. Right at the beginning of the Nazi era, a friend of H.D.'s had arrived at the train station and was prevented from crossing the street to the Deichmann house by a large carnivalesque crowd of howling people. Suddenly, a big open car drove by, carrying a group of Nazi bigwigs in dress uniform and an African potentate to whom they seemed quite deferential. My friend asked one of the onlookers what was happening. "Can't you see—they're turning into trained apes, just like at the circus!"

This is how the crowd made fun of the Nazis.

October 1989

Palais Deichmann 1868-1913

THE EYEGLASSES

To be precise, it wasn't *one* pair of glasses, but two: one belonging to an unknown man, and the other belonging to the chronicler, H.D. Fate had decreed it that way, back in late August of that ominous year 1939, three days before the war broke out. Even today, the question of who that bespectacled man was who played such a decisive role in H.D.'s life—possibly even saving it—remains a mystery. As the unknown man's glasses compelled him to follow the sergeant, all that could be seen of the bespectacled man was his back—quite a prosaic back. It would have been good to know what happened to him; but Fate had other plans.

H.D. and his wife had gone on vacation with their two small children and the maid from the Röhn whom they had grown close to—"leave" was the term used by the militaristic Germans when it concerned an employee of I.G. Farben. The family was staying in Switzerland with old friends, Hermann and Genia Schwarzwald, who had barely managed to escape Nazi Austria. While they were there, Hermann Schwarzwald died quite unexpectedly of a broken heart: driven out of the country he had served so well through the most important years of his life!

"You must go back to Germany! War will break out any moment now!" But H.D. and his wife wanted to stand by Genia Schwarzwald as long as possible, and so they delayed their departure until the 28th of August. Finally they had to part, almost surely forever (it must be remembered that the most simple communication with Jews abroad—by phone or letter—could be fatal).

The first leg of their journey took them to Ulm. They found it to be a summery town, but there was a noticeable lack of people on the streets; everyone was in search of an inner security that had been taken from them. There were few cars, because gas was now unavailable to private citizens. The town was still, a frightened hush lay on people's faces—in short, everyone awaited the inevitable disaster.

Night was falling, and the police ordered H.D. to drive with his lights dimmed—that is, using only the parking lights. Many times in the following six years H.D. was to drive with his lights totally off, but never again would it feel so uncanny, for later it became one of those realities of life to which one gets accustomed. And so they drove for many hours in the dark, almost alone on the Stuttgart-Frankfurt Autobahn. What was particularly frightening were the endless columns of military vehicles of every kind rolling toward them on the other side of the Autobahn. They seemed even darker than the few private cars on the road—like dreadful, dangerous, gigantic monsters that could on a whim swallow up everything. Were they phantoms without a destination? No! There was no doubt about it! This was already the march on France!

The children slept; the grown-ups dared not speak a word. They sighed with relief when they saw the sign for the Bad Homburg exit. It was a relief that was to be short-lived. Three more kilometers, and they had arrived. They were met at the door by the caretaker—their old seamstress—who was by now also part of the family. She was beside herself with worry. In her trembling hands she held draft papers calling up H.D. into the army. The authorities had come looking for him twice already, and now he had to report in person at eight o'clock sharp the next morning at the military recruiting office in Bad Homburg.

H.D. told himself: "If I hadn't delayed my return, I would have been a soldier by now." This first hesitation, as everyone in the family immediately realized, had borne precious fruit: a further night at home. So delay was the name of the game!

"I have no intention of showing up there in six hours half asleep! They don't know I'm back, so I'll take a sleeping pill (which H.D. never does), and forget everything for a few hours."

The next morning, he rigged himself out with the basic necessities he would need for the army, along with a Bible and a paperback of Goethe's *Faust*, and, his Swiss gasoline dwindling, set off to face his destiny.

The military recruiting office had set up shop in a side street by the spa gardens of Bad Homburg. When he pulled up next to the office, a major was standing on the balcony, and yelled down at him: "How dare you turn in a dirty vehicle!"

H.D. was outraged at being shouted at in this way, and feeling his anger flare up, yelled right back that he wasn't there to deliver his car but because of a draft summons that hadn't reached him, as he had just returned from abroad three hours ago! If they didn't need him he would gladly go back home immediately. The major wasn't used to being reprimanded by subordinates, and as is often the case with German officers, he immediately put his tail between his legs and asked H.D. in an almost conciliatory tone to "please" step into the office.

"Hm, yes, there is a draft summons for you, we might as well admit you right away."

"Impossible! Not only do I have to move my car, but I also have to report to my office in Frankfurt, which hasn't been notified that I'm being drafted, and hand over the war-effort projects I've been working on!"

"Fine, then report back to us at 1400 hours."

Another postponement—apparently an indication that further delaying tactics were in order! The long and the short of it was that H.D.'s colleagues at I.G. Farben expressed their sympathy, and sent him off with lots of good advice and all the best for his admission into the army. At home—the gas tank was by now critically low—H.D. discussed with his wife what was to be done.

Nothing!

Let Fate run its course . . . But no, not so fast. Up to this point, the delaying tactics had worked, so why not keep on delaying? "I won't report at 1400 hours—I'll report at 1600 hours!"

On this last trip his wife drove the car. There were several hundred civilians lined up in formation on the street outside the recruiting office.

"I'll stand on the corner and wave as you march by," his wife told him as they said goodbye.

H.D. got out of the car and walked over to a group of men standing in the background. These future soldiers had obviously not signed up yet, and he asked one of them whether his name had been called yet.

"Yes, a few times already. Why don't you go over there to the sergeant with the list."

"Thanks, I think I'll just stay here until my name's called out again!"

Initially nothing happened, but suddenly the sergeant came over to the group of unrecruited men with a portentous look in his eye.

"You lot! Go over there to the garden and await further orders!"

H.D.'s spirits sank. There was no sidestepping this time, so he went with the twenty or so men over to the garden. It was a turn-of-the-century garden: a gently sloping embankment behind the house, dotted with purposeless stones and hedges and a row of trees that ran all the way round. He sat down in the shade near the top of the embankment, his chest heavy. Fear of the inevitable began to grow inside him. He could see that the other men, in the same age-group as he—born between 1905 and 1910—were anything but enthusiastic about the prospect of going to war. They too were obviously worrying about themselves and their families. They had all come together once before, in the spring during the medical checkup, when they had been given a final inspection by the doctor—"Bend over!"—and then declared fit for service.

Everyone was still hoping not to be called, but it was clearly a false hope. A melancholy late summer calm hung in the air. Then the sergeant appeared again with a heavy stride.

"We've just released one of the men outside because of a leg injury. I want a volunteer to take his place!"

Silence. No one moved.

"In that case, you there!" he yelled at one of the men in the front row. A few minutes later, the tragedy repeated itself. Then came a long period of waiting that gave the men renewed hope, but this too was only a delusion.

"We need another volunteer!" Again no response. After three summons, the sergeant pointed at H. D.: "You with the glasses!" Wait, wait, let him call you again . . . after a couple

of drawn-out seconds, one of the men behind him stood up—
he too was wearing glasses—came down the embankment,
and walked off with the sergeant. All that could be seen of
him was his back.

A few minutes later, the men heard loud military orders
from the street and the sound of a large platoon marching
off. The sergeant appeared one last time: "The rest of you
can go home! You will receive a new draft notification in
three days!"

The rescued men got up slowly, like convalescents who
have not quite recuperated from a long illness, and left the
garden in a happy trance.

H.D.'s wife, standing on the street corner, was radiant
with happiness and disbelief when she saw him almost tot-
tering toward her with his little suitcase. Bemused and over-
joyed, she asked him what had happened . . . "I really have
no idea whether the sergeant meant me or the man behind
me—I guess I'll never know! Before the other man got up I
thought I was the only one there with glasses. I had no intention of doing him any wrong . . . but it's so good that I'm still
with you, who knows for how long. Now I can keep on fighting to stay away from the army."

That was the end of the eyeglasses, and a new lease on
life for their wearer.

The next morning, H.D. hurried to I. G. Farben, where
his colleagues eagerly listened to his story.

"Good that you're here! You can help us dig air-raid
ditches around the building!"

"Absolutely not! I'm going to be drafted in three days—
you can dig your own ditches!"

In the meantime, word went round that all draftees born
between 1907 and 1910 were to be sent to Poland to dig

trenches, and only later go into military training. H.D.'s employer came to the conclusion that H.D.'s civilian work—selling dyestuffs for I.G. Farben in Italy—was more important for the war effort, and consequently H.D. was released from active duty. The release remained in effect until March 1942 when a friend, who was a first lieutenant in the Frankfurt recruiting office, warned him a month in advance that his age group was no longer "releasable" from active duty.

H.D. began right away saying goodbye to his co-workers in the large I.G. Farben office-block, which housed over three thousand employees.

Two weeks later the phone rang.

"The G.B. Chem—the General Manager of Germany's four-year chemical production plan—is looking for someone who knows Italy and speaks Italian. I suggested you. It's all right with you, isn't it?" the director of the legal department asked.

As far as H.D. was concerned, it was most definitely all right! His services for the G.B. Chem lasted till the end of the war, and—again, luckily for H.D.—called for basically civilian work, which the chronicler will relate at a later point.

October 1989

Four Plates in Pieces

"*C'est sauvage, c'est sauvage!*" shouted the concierge, lungs bursting, at No. 5, Rue Villaret de Joyeuses—a small side street of the Avenue de la Grand Armeé in Paris. From July 1934 to June 1935, a newlywed couple, Dickie and H.D., lived on the fifth floor in a small furnished apartment they had draped with burlap to make it more to their taste.

It must have been around August 1934. The warm, still unpolluted evening air flowed gently through the attic window. Someone downstairs had left a motorbike running, and the drawn-out din was ruining the fascinating story a Dutch friend was telling about his life in China. It was getting dark, but everyone was too absorbed in the story to think of turning on the lights. Suddenly, H.D. jumped up, dashed into the kitchenette, grabbed a pot full of liquid, and hurled its contents in a cascade down on the motorbike . . . But it wasn't water, as H.D. had thought in the dark, it was milk. The milk not only splashed all over the bike, but also into the open car of the couple who lived next door. They had been following the whole scene from their window with considerable amusement. Dismayed, H.D. immediately offered to clean their car, but, laughing, they refused. They congratulated H.D. on the silence that resulted from his successful maneuver.

To get the all-important concierge back on his side, H.D.

had to fork out a number of small tips, offer profuse apologies, and keep smiling at her penitently. Without all the racket, the pieces might still be plates today. (It is quite unusual for broken pieces, as in this case, to have a positive outcome. However, even back then in Paris it was already quite clear that only after five years of war, with Europe "in broken pieces," would the Germans be brought back to their senses.) But before the modest milk-pouring incident, there were a few causally related events.

H.D. had been stationed in Paris by his firm, Frankfurt's I.G. Farben, and Dickie had joined him from Vienna that May, just in time to prepare everything for their long-planned wedding, which was to be held in early July. They could barely afford daily necessities, and even Dickie's mother, who was chaperoning her, was almost penniless. As a result, the number of wedding guests was extremely limited—ten, including the couple and the witness. H.D.'s Aunt Emma, who had lovingly supported her Cologne nephews since 1931, was coming all the way from London, and a church wedding was the least they could do for her. On July 5th, the Mayor of the 14th Arrondissement performed a civil service, and on July 7th the pastor of the German Evangelical Church in the Rue de Blanche performed a religious one. Construction workers were busily working nearby, and in order for the edifying words of the pastor to be heard, they were given a tip to stop hammering for half an hour.

The wedding reception took place at a summer restaurant west of Paris on the banks of the Seine, so close to the water that one could almost dip one's toes in it. It was a success in every way: the weather, everyone's good mood, the menu, the charming scenery. It is unclear how it happened that this restaurant was chosen—perhaps a friend had suggested it. However, its name was *Le Fruit défendu* (for the occasion, rebaptised *Le Fruit légalisé*). The restaurant consisted of many spacious, veranda-like *chambres séparées* each with a large private terrace overlooking the Seine, where we dined. But in the room, behind a large screen, stood a divan just scandalously large enough for a couple. H.D. only realized that the bed was there after all the arrangements for the reception had been made. He did not want to give up the beautiful scenery and the view of the river, so all that remained was to smuggle Aunt Emma past the bed, which in the end was quite easy once the screen was set up.

The wedding feast ended that evening at their apartment in the Rue Villaret de Joyeuses, where the couple leaned out of the aforementioned attic window to wave goodbye to H.D.'s brother Carl and Dickie's sister Jackie, both of whom had dressed up in formal wear to go dancing (in Paris!).

In late autumn of that same year, Genia Schwarzwald was H.D. and Dickie's first house guest. (There was a narrow couch in the small tube-like room facing the backyard, through which one could get to the fire escape.) Rudolf Serkin, the oldest of the "Schwarzwald children," had also arranged to be in Paris at the time. He had come to give a piano recital for German emigrés at the Quaker Meeting House. H.D. remembers the evening well. The recital took place in a small hall, and the lights were dimmed as Rudi played. The audience was made up almost exclusively of exiles—all one heard was German. Many were crying, overcome with emotion and gratitude. H.D. also wept; he, too, felt exiled, exiled from a world he had believed up to that point was progressive. There he was, with two friends who could no longer set foot in Germany. Things, they already suspected, would get worse, and this could only be overcome after Europe lay in broken pieces.

The day after the concert, Rudi came to the Rue Villaret de Joyeuses to have lunch with Genia Schwarzwald and was enchanted by everything, especially by the closeness and deep friendship that bound the four of them together. He rushed from one room to another, admired everything, looked out the windows, asked all kinds of questions, and listened with great amusement to the milk-rain story. Suddenly, he bumped against a pile of four plates, which Dickie had left standing on a small heater so that she could serve the food on warm plates.

The plates hesitated for a few seconds and then shattered into countless pieces on the floor. Rudi was mortified, but everyone else only laughed.

"Get over it!" H.D. said. "Or else I'll climb into the closet and cry very loudly!"

Rudi looked at H.D. with astonishment. "What do you mean, closet?"

"Yes, right by the entrance there's a large closet with a door that looks just like the door of a room, and one can go in there . . . and cry. When I have done something horrible to Dickie, or, worse, when she has done something horrible to me, I just lock myself in the closet and cry loudly."

H.D. showed him how, and Rudi was quite thrilled. "I want to try that!" Without further delay, he jumped into the closet, but his sobs were drowned out by everyone else's laughter. When he came out again he fell into six waiting arms that embraced him.

November 1989

BICYCLES

It is not surprising that many of the bicycles owned by the chronicler would have quite a few tales to tell. Three of their tales are as follows.

The Bicycle in Rome (1942-43)

From mid-March 1942, H.D. was a "drafted civilian," which meant that he was sworn-in like a soldier but not in uniform and not on active military service. He had three superiors: at the very top was the infamous Professor Carl Krauch, the G.B. Chem—chief of special chemical projects in Reichsmarshal Göring's four-year plan—who, after the war, was called to account for everything but knew of nothing. Then came H.D.'s actual section chief, Colonel Kirschner, who managed after the war to turn himself effortlessly from a Nazi opportunist into a profiteer in the mass-marketing of bras. Third in line was his chief clerk, a dangerous Nazi who on April 24, 1945, fled from Milan to Bolzano in a stolen car filled to the brim with loot.

H.D. reported for duty to this clerk on March 24, 1942, taking on the position of representative of the G.B. Chem in Italy. Everything had been prepared at the office even before anyone knew who this representative was going to be, and H.D. could barely hide his astonishment when he found himself on the top floor of a building which housed the Nazi office for labor recruitment. This former branch of the Labor Ministry of the German Reich had been exclusively engaged, since well before the war and right up to September 8, 1943, in recruiting and transporting voluntary laborers to Germany. It was only after the Italian cease-fire, when there were no more voluntary laborers to be found, that the office developed an interest in forced labor.

What does all this have to do with H.D.'s bicycle? (That eternal problem of curbing the reader's impatience!) Up to this point, H.D. had been a bona-fide civilian. This was the first time he found himself within the sphere of a Nazi commission—actually becoming, overnight, a representative of one! He did not know how he would deal with this new

development, but there was one thing he decided right on the spot: he was going to do everything in his power not to be thrown into the same pot with the labor recruiters or any of the other Nazi commissions in Rome. His new appointment brought with it the option of a car with official licence plates. But the last thing H.D. wanted was for the locals to say: "Look, here comes another Nazi!" And anyway, his work didn't actually require a car. It became clear right away that his only commute would be from his hotel at the end of Via Sistina (Trinità dei Monti) to his office in Trastevere, and from there to Piazza S.S. Apostoli (Piazza Venezia), where the Federation of the Building and Construction Industry was located, which was working in conjunction with his commission. Only rarely did he have to travel to other offices in the center of Rome. So he decided to get himself a bicycle instead of a car.

By the third year of the war, Nazi bureaucracy had reached a point where even ordering a nail had become an uncertain venture. So H.D. hesitantly asked his Roman business partners how one could get hold of a bicycle. You simply buy one, they answered smiling, and a pretty young Roman co-worker was given the task of securing one for him. She obliged, and afterward eagerly showed the cyclist all the beauties of Rome.

Nowadays when one describes the old Rome of the Seven Hills as a paradise for pedestrians and cyclists, one runs the risk of losing credibility. No traffic jams, hardly a car, all goods transported by horse-drawn carts—leaving winsome aromas everywhere. Even back then there were overcrowded trams and buses, but they did not cut into the beauty of the city. The air was so pure, and there was a constant warm breeze. Very rarely, there were heavy downpours that covered the hills of the city with mountain streams. But then the brilliant rays of the sun only shone brighter. Everywhere there were well-tended parks, everywhere flowers, all in a motley sea of small houses and larger buildings, their pastels clashing with the brighter colors of the flowers. What was most overwhelming for a northerner like H.D. was Rome's unbridled light—the sharp yet unaggressive contours never ceased to amaze him.

H.D. had known Rome as a tourist, and his civilian work had taken him there for a few days a number of times. But to actually live in Rome was something quite different. Every morning he jumped onto his bicycle at Trinità dei Monti and let himself fly down Via Gregoriana. He had to brake so he could make a right turn and continue downhill to get to the main post office in Piazza San Silvestro. There, on the evening of July 25, 1943—after Mussolini's arrest—they had refused to dispatch H.D.'s celebratory but alas insufficiently cryptic telegram to his wife: "Never received so well!" (Censorship was still in full force.) From the post office he would ride over to Piazza Colonna, where on April 7, 1926 (he was barely nineteen at the time), he had watched Mussolini, a big bandage on his nose, being driven out of the gates of the Palazzo Chigi. An Irish woman's gunshot had missed its mark by a few millimeters. From there, H.D. would ride past the Pantheon, which always inspired feelings of reverence and awe in him, and then on to the Forum Argentina and over the Garibaldi Bridge to Viale del Re number 1, (renamed Viale Trastevere).

Leaving his bicycle at the entrance, he would go up to his office on the top floor. There, from a large terrace, a staggering panorama of Rome unfolded: in front, the Isola Tiberina, to the right, the Aventino, and far away to the left, the dome of San Pietro.

But one didn't have to look far to be distracted from the charade of deep immersion in work. To the left, across the road which led to Santa Maria in Trastevere, there was a nunnery, on the roof of which the novices, after hanging out the washing, would play ball. Their black habits billowed in the wind, conjuring up images of Carpaccio's painting in Venice of monks fleeing from a lion. Obviously, even the novices were allowed to brighten the severity of their lives for a few minutes.

In Piazza Santa Maria in Trastevere, which was within walking distance, there was a trattoria called Galassi, which after the war unfortunately became elegant. Back in those days, it was partitioned into two sections. One entered through a sort of wine-bar that was always chock-full of Trastevians, coachmen, construction workers, sextons, market women, all good and kind people, who warmly greeted the regular customers passing through to the dining alcoves in the other section. In the evenings, an old accordion-player and an even older guitarist played local music so beautifully that they were cheered on with a shower of tips from the diners. On two occasions H.D. brought along sedate German orchestra conductors, who listened to the musicians enthusiastically even after an evening of classical music. H.D.'s co-workers always had lunch there. The local atmosphere and the wine of the Roman hills successfully managed for a little while to disperse the dire world situation.

One of the main attractions was the many traditional wine-delivery vehicles that now no longer exist: high carts with gigantic wheels, pulled by diminutive horses. In the old days, it was only because of these wheels that the carts could be dragged through the deep mud and sand of the villages to reach the papal city. Small barrels, about ninety centimeters high and thirty centimeters wide, were stacked up high on the flat and narrow cart, the height of the pile depending on whether the barrels were full or empty, their weight distributed so that the cart shafts pulled the horse up instead of weighing it down. The driver sat on one side of the shaft crossbar right behind the horse's swishing tail (swatting at mosquitoes?), leaning back and forth to keep the load balanced.

Thirty years later, friends called the cyclist to account about his state of mind back then, and he wrote: *". . . an impossible venture today (1976), because everyone's state of political awareness has changed so drastically, both at the individual and the collective levels. On the one hand, ideological differentiations have today become clearer, but, on the other, the positions of the individuals within them are less personal, more standardized. I, a person not any different from anyone else, was constantly on the lookout for a better world, a state of mind I still hold to. It never crossed my mind that we might not ultimately see one. So, I was constantly on the prowl for signs that things were about to turn out for the better. A Nazi who behaved honorably— who didn't, for instance, denounce people—could make me ecstatic: it proved that even someone who had been led astray could have elements of goodness in them!*

I was never a moralist and, on my bicycle and otherwise, always enjoyed everything that Rome had to offer— without a bad conscience, but also without trying to elude the confrontation with the horror of what was happening, and without suppressing my critical consciousness and my readiness to bear a share of the responsibility. Later, I tried to find explanations for my two-facedness. But none satisfied me and I always ended up asking myself questions like:

Could I have endured the world back then without also try-ing to some extent to enjoy that world, without deeply rel-ishing it? Was my enjoyment a form of compensation for the horrendous things one had to live with, to live through? Or was I simply too young to be able to reject the pleasures that offered themselves to me? Or was my awareness too limited, too underdeveloped, to comprehend what was really going on in the world? This last question I must answer with a definite NO! And that is what still baffles me. Within me there was an amalgam of a distressing clarity of vision and a (deliberately?) limited awareness. But that was not true either, because one had no qualms of doing everything in one's power to impede evil, or at least to ease it."

Directly opposite the office building, the sidewalk wid-ened into a small square where there was a kiosk, and within close aromatic range stood a *vespasiano*. These were public urinals—naturally only for men—named after the Roman Emperor who had invented them in order to at least limit the stench of urine to certain street corners. These little piss-houses were built so that one could see everything that was going on inside except for the actual body parts involved. There were two large tin stalls across from each other, one opening to the left, and one to the right, with a curved screen-like entrance. The tin walls were ornamentally perforated on top and on the bottom, so that down below one could see the perpetrator's patiently waiting feet, while above you could see him dreamily gaze into the distance.

One day in the spring of 1943, a group of construction workers suddenly appeared. Within a few hours the kiosk had been relocated to the other side of the street and the venerable *vespasiano* razed to the ground. A wooden fence was put up around the wounded sidewalk, and an official

War Ministry notice informed passers-by that a public air-raid shelter was being planned, a scheme that never came to pass as the Allies landed in Sicily soon after. Within a few days the stagnant construction project had lost its attraction. But a lone *vespasiano* devotee was so bound to this time-worn place of relief that he still appeared on the scene every morning at the same time. He scampered with difficulty up a gravel mound, the stones slipping under his heels, till he reached the top slat of the fence. There he swung both legs over and slid down the pile of sand on the other side. A few more unsteady steps and he reached his goal, exposed himself, and let the relieving stream that he had been hoarding flow free. He then carefully tucked away his lightened member and set off on the arduous task of climbing the fence again. H.D. and his secretary were highly amused by this moving scenario and laughed at the persistence and stubbornness of mankind. But their lighthearted laughter was quickly chilled by the thought that there would be war as long as there were gravel mounds by wooden fences.

Until May 1943, H.D. had a distant relative living in Rome. Her name was Vera von Bergen, and she was married to the former German ambassador to the Vatican. Her daughter from her first marriage had more or less grown up with H.D. and his family, but an unexpected blemish had developed: she had become one of the leaders of the Nazi German Girls' Organization. Courteous shyness on both sides of the family prohibited any mention of the matter. The daughter is irrelevant to the story, except for the fact that because of her H.D. got to know her mother, who had remained wholly untouched by Nazi ideology. H.D. became a frequent guest at the ambassadorial residence, where the doorman greeted the cyclist and his bicycle with invariable fatherly warmth.

In 1943, H.D. had been sent to I.G. Farben's construction site at Auschwitz on official business four times, and his
horrified quest for ways to stop the crimes there left him no
peace. He had heard that Vera von Bergen had free access to
Pope Pius XII. H.D. asked to see her in Rome. She immediately agreed to have lunch with him at the Casina Valadier
(March 4, 1943). As he had expected, she knew little if anything about the horrors that had been taking place for a year
at Auschwitz. Vera von Bergen fully agreed with him on his
stance . . . but she could not see how she could possibly ask
the pope to stand up before the world and publicly excommunicate Hitler. H.D. convinced her that the war would be
considerably shortened as a result of such a move, but couldn't
convince her that it was her duty to actively take a stand.
Most likely she was aware that Pius XII's anti-communism
overshadowed everything, even his duty as the guardian of
the Ten Commandments.

The meeting was a disappointment, and she tried to lift
H.D.'s spirits by inviting him to a luncheon at the embassy in
honor of Foreign Secretary Ciano and Mussolini's daughter,
his wife. Ciano sat there smiling, not suspecting that nine
months later Hitler would order his father-in-law to shoot
him. H.D. took part in this hangman's luncheon without coming to feel that he had sat at the table with world figures. The
notorious SS Dollmann was also present. So there was enough
to mull over . . . and to smile at bitterly, when H.D. thought
of the lunch at the Casina Valadier nine days earlier. Whether
the hostess's slightly apologetic smile is a historic truth, or
merely wishful thinking on the chronicler's part, is no longer
verifiable.

I.G. Farben's Board of Directors had managed after 1938
to secure permission from the Nazis to allow one of the Jewish

co-founders of the firm to live on a comfortable retirement allowance in Rome. But in the autumn of 1942, Berlin disallowed any further monetary transfers to the co-founder, and H.D. suggested to one of the board members that payments could be made through the director of a small factory that belonged to I.G. Farben in Milan.

"I take it that you do understand why I would prefer to avoid putting such an order through," the board member answered. "You take care of it!" And H.D. took care of it.

On July 9th, H.D. went to a small dinner party thrown by Colombo, a building contractor who had a villa at Subiaco near the Simbruini hills southeast of Rome. Colombo was very clever at reconciling managerial interests with political independence. H.D. does not recall where Colombo's six guests spent the night, but he does remember that things were quite lively, even though the atmosphere became increasingly tense in the face of decisive events that were about to take place. And the events *did* take place. Throughout the night, someone sat and listened secretly to Radio London. In the morning, word finally came that the British had landed in Sicily and that the few Germans on the scene had been incapable of convincing the uninterested Italians to set up a defense force. Colombo's guests rushed back to Rome . . .

According to his pocket diary, the German cyclist actually spent that day, a Saturday, cycling along the banks of Lake Albano, a fact that he cannot explain to himself even to this day!

On July 25th, H.D. returned from official business in Germany. His train was stopped at the stazione Tiburtina in Rome—why, nobody knew. But he found a taxi that took him past the blacked-out center of town to his hotel on the Via Sistina. He checked in as usual and went up to his room on the fifth floor. The room looked out onto a balcony that was more of a canopy over the fourth floor. From there one could see the whole city over the roof of the Hertziana, all the way to San Pietro. It was a very warm evening; H.D. threw open the French windows and rushed out half-dressed onto the balcony to drink in the Roman night air. Hundreds of cheering voices rose from the blackened city. H.D. had never heard anything like it. Deeply moved, he quickly threw on his clothes and ran downstairs to find out what had happened. "Haven't you heard? The king has had Mussolini arrested!" H.D. rushed over to Piazza Colonna, where large crowds of people were swaying back and forth shouting anti-Fascist and anti-German war cries. As the reader already knows, H.D. tried in vain to send a joyful telegram to his wife, and so, wrapped in thought, he returned to his hotel. But his joy soon turned into fear at what might come next, what might happen to him and his family. He didn't doubt that *for* Italy the war had ended—though he couldn't imagine that *in* Italy the Nazi murdering would continue all around him for two more years.

Within two days, orders came from Berlin: "Destroy everything—send all important files to Berlin!"

The cyclist went on his last bicycle ride through Rome on August 2nd, carrying an umbrella.

Why does he remember the umbrella? That afternoon H.D. had returned to his hotel which, up to that point, had been free of Germans, and found to his chagrin the whole reception area chock-full of German naval officers. Here, too, one could feel the tension in the air. A casual German acquaintance pulled him to the side and told him: "Word has come from Florence that Hitler's dead!" Transported, the cyclist grabbed his acquaintance and began dancing with joy, triumphantly waving his umbrella. His friend stopped him in terror. "No! No! Are you mad? If the news is wrong, you're finished!" H.D. stopped dead in his tracks.

The chronicler left Rome on August 3rd, 1943, entrusting his beloved bicycle to the beautiful Roman woman who had helped him secure it.

Six crazed weeks followed H.D.'s departure from Rome, until the colonel finally fled with him into "friendly"—that is, German-occupied—Italian territory. The G.B. Chem's state of mind was no less muddled than Italy's state of affairs. Since no one knew what to do with H.D., he was sent home on an eighteen-day leave.

Italy surrendered to the allies on September 8, 1943. Goebbels told the German people a day later, but H.D., who at the time was on a train from Frankfurt to Berlin, had no clue. Berlin was already blacked out as the train pulled into the station, and H.D. hurried across the street to the offices of the G.B. Chem, where the porter was supposed to tell him where he could spend the night. He entered through the large gate into a big hall, expecting his reverberating "HEIL-HITLER" to be returned. There was no answer. In the far corner he noticed three men bent over a newspaper. He barked out a second "HEILHITLER," and they looked up in some confusion. H.D. asked them what was going on, and, surprised, they asked him if he didn't know that Italy had signed a cease-fire.

"Great!" H.D. blurted out.

"What do you mean, 'great'?"

H.D. realized instantly that he was in for it, and launched in on a lengthy justification. He had been working for the G.B. Chem two years now in Italy, and therefore knew first-hand that Italy was no more than a dead weight tied to

Germany's leg. Germany had to send everything to Italy, and not just German soldiers who were so desperately needed elsewhere. The Italian armed forces were useless—that had been painfully obvious during the Allied landing in Sicily. Trust the Italians, and you're lost! And so on and so forth—so, Italy's leaving Germany's side is a true blessing. The Führer had surely expected more from them, it must have been a harsh blow to him. The discussion—actually, the monologue—ended with everyone agreeing with H.D., which led him to hope that they would not see him as one of those "defeatists" who were to be immediately denounced to the Gestapo. After an uneasy night, his fears were only relieved when his colleagues asked him what his predictions for future developments in Italy were . . . nobody referred to the previous night's joyous outcry.

The End-of-the-war-and-early-postwar bicycle

The reader might expect that the three bicycles followed each other in quick succession. That, however, was only the case for the first two, and even between them there had been a short four-wheel interlude.

In the winter of 1944, in gratitude for interceding for him with the Germans, an Italian acquaintance had taken the chronicler to a black-market source where H.D. bought the most important bicycle of his life. Before he could purchase it, three more bicycles managed to "convince" as many German officers. The chronicler relishes the memory of such events to this day.

In San Giovanni Lupatoto, just south of Verona, friends of H.D. owned a large leather-supply factory that produced everything from insulation material to luggage, to all kinds of containers. By December 1944, the owners were afraid that the receding Italian front would destroy their factory, and they wanted to bring at least their stock to safety. So they asked H.D. if there was any way he could arrange for a German army-truck convoy to transport their treasures to Milan. Arranging something like that wasn't quite as simple as it might seem. The first step was to find out if there was a transport unit stationed anywhere near Milan or Verona (it turned out that there was a unit in Colà, about five kilometers north of Peschiera, comfortably holed up in an old castle). The next step was to be introduced to the commanding officer as someone high up in the war effort and convince him of the importance of the freight—vital war material that must on no account fall into enemy hands. By then H.D. was sure the war was coming to an end. All it would take was a final battle near Verona, where the Germans would once more act as heroically as they had done until then—energetically blowing up all kinds of bridges as they retreated, including pedestrian bridges, as they did with the Roman bridge in Verona. By now the chronicler no longer felt he was standing on official ground and enjoyed the idea of wrestling a huge military convoy away from its real duties and make it work for his Italian friends.

On December 22, 1944, H.D. finally managed to push the German officers (in his pocket diary he had written "pigheads") into action, and they finally declared themselves ready to transport the important war material. This, however, only came about after H.D. pulled three bicycles out of his hat: The date and time of the transport were suddenly agreed upon. Nobody said what the bicycles were actually for. But although everyone spoke of Germany's great final victory, the bicycles, if push came to shove, might well come in handy for a quick getaway. In the castle yard the bicycles were quickly unloaded from the roof rack of the Lancia-Augusta. There followed a quick "See you in San Giovanni in mid-February"—and that was that!

On February 11, 1945, two-and-a-half months before the end of the war, two convoys, each made up of eight trucks, materialized, much to everyone's surprise. The second convoy was already being loaded when H.D. turned up for inspection. Everyone was in the very best of moods, especially the somewhat elderly German truckdrivers—the factory had provided large amounts of wine, countless salamis, and heaps of Verona-grown tobacco.

The following day, H.D. discovered that one of the trucks had slid into an embankment because of the icy roads. Only one, however, and its freight was already being transferred to a replacement truck.

Before the second bicycle came onto the scene, three long and tragic months went by—tragic also for the Germans, who could not be kept from continuing their horrendous crimes till the very last moment.

On April 25, the German troops in Milan finally retreated, leaving the road open for the partisans.

From April 26th on, H.D.'s bicycle remained by his side, not only as a means of transportation, but as a concrete symbol of a regained freedom that had been almost completely forgotten. One no longer had to keep a frightened eye out for German guards and patrols. The cyclist who, up to that point, had acted to the best of his ability as a protector, now turned into a protection-seeker. As a matter of fact, it wasn't so much that he himself sought protection, as that his Italian friends forced their protection on him. Giustizia e Libertà furnished him with a photo I.D. he has kept to this day. In the first few days after the liberation, his friends cautioned him not to go outside at all, advice he only followed after dark. He didn't venture far beyond Via Gesù 8, where he was staying with his friends the de Finettis. But on the day of the great celebration, a few days after the "Liberazione"—it must have been the 27th or 28th of April—the partisans came marching from the Corso Vittorio Emanuele into Piazza del Duomo and were greeted by hundreds of thousands of cheering people. H.D. stood all alone near the entrance of the Galleria and wept—overcome by the feeling of freedom and happiness that surged from the crowd. He felt the strain of the last twelve years begin to lift, but he was at a loss. A vast emptiness opened up inside him. He realized that he had managed to survive, almost with integrity; almost, because when it came down to it he should not have survived, but been a victim of the Nazis like all the others. This "wrong" was something he had to carry with him into the future. At that point his imagination could in no way foresee the pleasures and disappointments that this would bring.

One of the most immediate pleasures was the feeling that he belonged to the winning side. Few could understand his attitude, least of all the high-ranking British officers H.D. met at the house of his friend Ferré. But it also happened that people more or less overlooked the fact that they had a German standing in front of them. Once his former Italian colleagues even commissioned him to meet with the economic director of the C.N.L., the National Liberation Committee, to contend that the representation of the former I.G. Farben in Italy should fall to a private corporation and not to the state. But the provisional director politely declined to meet with a German, even when he came with such good references—and furthermore, it had been already decided to integrate the I.G. Farben office into a state-owned company.

Most of H.D.'s cycling in those days had the express goal of securing as quickly as possible a permit to return to his family in the American occupied zone. But no guidelines had yet been set for transporting civilians back to Germany—and no guidelines were to be expected before the Potsdam Conference. Even the British sergeant in Via Telesio, who ordered H.D. to knock before he entered his office—and then was startled at how fast he turned on his heel, left the room, knocked on the door, and reentered—had no idea how H.D. could get back to Germany. There was also no way to send a message home or to receive one.

One fine morning in May, H.D. went for a bicycle ride to the northern part of town with a German woman he had worked with. (As Germans, they had to stay within the city limits.) They went to a trattoria in the suburbs and slipped off to a table in the far corner of the garden, so that speaking to each other in soft Italian, no one would notice them. But the motherly landlady came rushing up to the table. "You're Germans, right?" H.D. and his former colleague diffidently nodded their heads. "Oh, I had such nice German soldiers who used to come here! Do you know how I can find out where they are? They were such nice boys, and I'm worried they might be suffering somewhere in some prison camp!" How nice that not all Germans were remembered with bitterness.

H.D. had cycled through Milan for three months before learning that he could get permission to be transported back to Germany along with other "displaced persons," from a camp that had been set up in an area between Bolzano and

Merano. But when the transports would start, nobody knew.

H.D.'s pocket diary reads: "August 6th, the F.S.S. (Field Security Services) finally granted me permission after waiting for 1½ hr. to leave Milan . . . after a vehement argument with Captain Kane in the Questura. Also secured a permit to travel to Bolzano."

On August 7, H.D. traveled to San Giovanni Lupatoto, and from there he left the following day for Bolzano, his bicycle tied to the roof of his car. H.D.'s good friend Stangalini accompanied him in a car with a two-wheeled contraption in tow. On it a strange coal-burning device had been set-up to produce the necessary fuel. They made it to Bolzano, but only because the driver was an expert in this soon-to-be obsolete gas substitute and knew exactly when to stop and throw more coals on the fire.

In Bolzano, there was another long wait. H.D. presented himself at the camp for displaced persons and managed to arrange things so that he wouldn't have to stay there. "I fought the Nazi regime for twelve years, and now I'm to be locked up in a camp full of them? I would be grateful if you could spare me that and allow me to take lodgings in town while I'm waiting for the train. My Italian friends will pay for my room and board." The commander in charge of the camp saw H.D.'s point and granted him permission. He promised to have him transported to Germany on the first train out.

His pocket diary entry for August 10th reads: "Bolzano Questura: Registered at the camp. Stay in town confirmed. Overnight at Hotel 'Under the Stars'."

His entry for August 29th: "Major Geddas confirms: departure tomorrow." The day after at 9:00 H.D. had to report to the camp. The itinerary: 1:20 p.m., transportation to the station—2:30 p.m., confirm seat—free afternoon in town until 5 p.m.—7:30 p.m., departure.

The train was made up of freight cars with open doors. There were approximately thirty passengers per car, all of them Nazis. H.D. managed to secure a place by the wall, his bicycle hung on a large hook over his head. In the dark from time to time, he ran his fingers over it. The train went with lighting speed: It took only three and a half hours to reach the Brenner Pass! There he had to wait three and a half hours in the rain for the train from the "other side." In the meantime, H.D. moved up to the position of German-English translator, which only really began to pay-off at the old German border, for the Brenner Pass and Innsbruck were occupied by the French. When the train arrived the American officer in charge of the border crossing in Mittenwald was at a complete loss. He hadn't been informed that there would be one, nor what it was transporting. He had absolutely no idea what to do and finally begged that we proceed to Munich. That was perfectly fine with us! The train arrived in Munich at 7 p.m., after having stopped by a large meadow outside the city so that the travelers could freshen up. A wide-open meadow lined with two hundred pee-ers and pee-ettes—a vista H.D. will never forget! But let us get back to the situation at hand.

In the heavily damaged train station in Munich, no one knew anything of the "train from Italy." With H.D. in the lead, the passengers went looking for an American officer, who also had no idea about transporting German civilians. After a few phone calls, he told everyone to go over (without guards!) to Hitler's "House of German Art." From there, they would be moved to a camp on the banks of the Chiemsee and then, after inspection, be sent to their homes (it was to take another six weeks). "Without guards!"—that was too good to be true, and H.D. decided then and there to break away from his fellow travelers and leave them without a translator.

A former colleague had given him the address of her sister in case he needed help. The sister took him in and the following day even managed to secure a travel pass for him from the C.I.C. office where she worked. But the pass was not valid for the army train north, which was reserved exclusively for Americans and the Germans working for them. H.D. was advised that he should take an empty coal train which was due to leave from the freight yard in Laim. It was forbidden, of course, but one could always hide . . . The train was made up of empty open coal wagons and left at 5:30 p.m. on its way to the Ruhr. H.D. traveled only as far as Hanau: his friends had warned him to change trains there. Already in Augsburg it looked as if his luck was about to run out. The train stopped at a passenger station, and for well over an hour American guards marched up and down the platform to stop civilians from climbing on. H.D. and two traveling companions sat glued to the car wall, almost flat against the floor like H.D.'s bicycle, frightened that they might be seen from the platform on the other side. Fate spared them from a second group of guards.

Then out of the ashes came an unexpected blessing. It turned out that in Hanau a place was available in an overcrowded passenger train that was to leave an hour and a half later for Friedberg. H.D. does not remember how he managed to accommodate his bicycle, but he remembers well enough the bitter disappointment when he arrived in Friedberg: the hope that he would bicycle home that same night was immediately crushed. There was a curfew until six in the morning, and the American guards, though happy to talk to a German in their own language, were not to be moved. So H.D. had to brave the waiting room for the next seven hours.

The waiting room stood witness to the appalling squalor of the first postwar months in Germany: broken windows everywhere, mountains of dirt and rubbish, rickety makeshift benches with people crammed together atop one another, like on the jam-packed trains. It was hard to tell them apart. There were returning soldiers, refugees from the East and from bombed-out cities, foreign laborers of every description, mothers and children searching for relatives, smokers everywhere— an indescribable cloud of vapors hung in the air. Everyone was dying to tell of the horrors they had lived through, and you felt that the least you could do for these poor destitute creatures clutching desperately at straws was to listen to their stories. All night, H.D. heard tales of woe. There was one advantage, however, in listening to these people: he soon had no strength left to fear what the future—which he would have to face in a few hours—had in store for him.

On the fourth day of his departure from Bolzano, just before 6 a.m., H.D. managed to talk the guards into letting him go. He climbed on his bicycle—a most precious object as the reader will by now agree—and set off on his way home. The closer he got to his goal, the faster he pedaled. He finally arrived. His house stood undamaged before him, and in it everyone was still asleep. All he wrote that day in his pocket diary was: "Lunch with the Hartners."

For a while the precious bicycle remained the only mode of transportation through the rubble of the city, as well as the only mode of communication, in those days almost more important than food.

The Milan bicycle

"All good things come in threes!" Even if the third bicycle did not take part in any dramatic events, it did have an important function: it enriched the cyclist's life after he moved into town and, provided that it didn't rain, served as a means of transportation to work every day. For a while now, H.D. had been working as the *consigliere delegato* (a sort of chairman of the board) of a marketing company which distributed German chemical products. This made his cycling through town somewhat of an oddity. In those days it was still a pleasure to cycle through Milan, but H.D. also enjoyed the conceit that once on his bicycle, he no longer belonged to the professional class. But let's move on before things get too complicated. His way to school, as he called it, took him through the Parco Sempione, and then over a bridge that crossed the tracks leading north to the lakes. On the other side of the tracks, by a row of trees, a group of charming ladies relentlessly exercised their profession, which one would generally expect them to do only at night. The same women were there every day. H.D. knew them all, and as business was relatively slow, they exchanged pleasantries.

Eventually the Milan bicycle departed as well, but not because H.D. had been commissioned to leave town, or even the country. It just so happened that years later, a careless friend borrowed the bicycle (without H.D.'s permission) and left it standing seductively unattended on a Mediterranean beach in the sun. It was stolen.

But before this tragedy occurred, the chronicler would like to quickly relate one of the most successful rides of the third bicycle. The cyclist and his office friends believed that it was important to get together and celebrate whenever an occasion arose—otherwise life would be too dull. One of the things they did was to organize a large Christmas party for the children in the mensa, a kind of canteen in the large company warehouse. The cyclist had the idea of dressing up as Santa Claus and cycling past the 100-meter-long warehouse with a large sack of presents on his shoulder. The closer he came to the gate, the louder the children cheered as they crowded to the windows.

But Santa Claus was not only kindness personified, he also had a bit of the devil in him. About twenty meters before he reached the entrance, he did an about-face and pretended to pedal in the opposite direction. The children's cheers turned into loud wails audible all the way down the street. Touched, Santa Claus turned his bicycle around, and rode back to the ramp, where he delivered the large sack of presents.

March 1990

THE KAISER'S GOLD TABLEWARE

At the beginning of October 1943 H.D. was ordered to return to Rome. An automobile was his only means of transportation, and the struggle for repairs, tires, and gas took up a large part of the day. H.D.'s pocket diary for October 9th reads, "Gas at last," while "Drive to Rome with Nando Ferré settled" had already been entered on October 7th.

On October 10th they drove by way of Pavia—where they were to load up with provisions for friends in Rome—to a lady friend of Ferré's in Pesaro. H.D., who of course was left empty-handed, noted in his diary: "Effort great, result not completely convincing; true rapport with Italy lacking," which leads one to infer the charming lady's foreign status.

The day after his arrival in Rome, H.D., as the representative of the Ministry of Armaments' chemical division, took part for the first time in a RuK meeting (*Rüstung und Kriegsproduktion*, "Armament and War Production") presided over by General Becht, head of the military administration. As in similar meetings over the following months, the general first reported on the conditions of the access roads. These had been bombed the previous day, but had been made passable again by the TODT Organization, the military construction task force. In order to defend the city by arms against the approaching Allies, there was some discussion of depriving Rome of the status of "open city," granted to the Vatican by all combatants. Since mounting such a defense would be impossible with the access roads destroyed, Ferré and H.D. decided to "pass along" information about their condition the same day as the RuK meetings. Ferré would wait until the end of a meeting in H.D.'s car, in front of the Albergo Città. H.D. would drive Ferré to a different street corner near the Vatican each evening, where Ferré would vanish into the darkness and reappear a few minutes later, always highly satisfied. This led General Becht to remark at the next meeting about the fiendishly good spy network of the enemy.

Their mission accomplished, Ferré and H.D. considered they had earned the splendid *pastasciutta* of the celebrated chef "Alfredo" (long live the black market!). Kaiser Wilhelm II in his time relished Alfredo's cooking so much that he had some gold tableware (a fork and spoon) presented to him as a memento. Thereafter it was proudly exhibited to all the guests, including his two eager friends in the wartime winter of 1943-44.

H.D.'s office consisted of a single room at the labor service headquarters. Under these close circumstances it was quite normal for him to participate in the deliberation on how to carry out an order from Berlin to round up all Italian men in Rome and forcibly transport them to the Reich as workers in the armaments industry—something to be prevented at all costs.

H.D. asked to speak at the meeting. He began by appreciating the wisdom of the order from Berlin, but expressed some concerns. Adequate transportation certainly did not exist. The roads were not fit to accommodate the men on foot (the railway was only functioning from Chiusi onward). There would surely be difficulties—perhaps insuperable—with provisions, sanitation, and last but not least, the police guarding thousands of men thinking of nothing but escape. Therefore, the operation should be limited to truly able-bodied men, and to find them, a census would first have to be taken. The others turned on H.D. with indignation: his proposal was tantamount to disobeying an order of the Führer. As to how they proposed to overcome the difficulties he had enumerated, no one quite knew. With that, the exchange ended. Because he was the only one who spoke Italian, H.D. was charged with delivering to the municipal registry office the order to take a census.

The registry office was located at the foot of the Aventine, in a barracks-like building behind the Church of Santa Maria in Cosmedin, famous because La Bocca della Verità is situated in its portico. A face is chiseled in a large, round, flat stone resembling a millstone. The mouth of this curious piece is said not to release the hand of a liar who dares insert it. One might suppose that everyone has always told the truth, for up till now no one knows of any hand trapped there, though Kurt Waldheim is said to have pulled his out just in time.

Slowly, meditating on the Verità, H.D. climbed up to the fourth floor, where the director of the registry office received him with the deference due then to Germans. At his visitor's request, the director summoned his most important colleagues. As the orders of the German civil administration were explained to them, their faces changed color, and in the end, showed naked despair. Taking a census was completely out of the question. There was nothing left, no reliable census-takers, no paper, not even a press where the forms could be printed. After half an hour, H.D. appeared resigned, but asked the director for a word in private. "We are alone, without witnesses," H.D. said. "You can't denounce me, and I can't denounce you. You haven't understood at all what's going on. Even if it's only a fictitious census, it would prevent the otherwise unavoidable suffering of countless numbers of your people. The longer the census takes, the better. Meanwhile, not a single person will get dragged off, and in three months at the most, the Allies will be here!" The director turned pale, then red, then pale again. He stammered a few words of apology and stood up. He offered his hand to H.D. and promised solemnly to try to do his best. In fact, they were still taking the census when the Allies occupied Rome, two months later than H.D. had predicted.

Pleased with himself, H.D. left the registry office, not suspecting that there would be a dangerous epilogue. The following day, he and the head of the labor office were summoned before Consul-General Eitel Friedrich Möllhausen, at that time the plenipotentiary of the German ambassador in Salò. He accused H.D. point-blank of sabotage and was now going to hand over the case to the SS. H.D. concealed his rage with difficulty and replied: "Then you'll have to come with me, because you are under suspicion of wanting to make all military movement impossible by your insistence on reducing the city to chaos with this roundup." Möllhausen froze and, after the head of the labor office assured him that H.D. was an exemplary patriot totally dedicated to victory, the consul-general did not persist in his threat. After the war, this same Möllhausen claimed he had helped the partisans in Rome!

A few days later, a man came to the labor office with the offer of a "chemical invention that would change the course of the war" and was sent to H.D., the representative of the chemical division. In answer to the question, "Are you really an Italian, or a German Nazi?" (he did not know a word of German), he stuttered indignantly that he was Italian. "Then it's your patriotic duty to let the Germans lose the war without your help." Dumbfounded, he too changed color several times, and stammered something incomprehensible. He left the blueprints with H.D. and walked out in confusion without saying a word. The next morning, H.D. was summoned to the head of the labor office, where he faced a high-ranking SS officer with a severe expression. "Is it true that you said these things to the inventor yesterday?" "Of course I did. I considered the man a swindler and wanted to provoke him. All the same, I reported to Berlin immediately." For an SS man, the whole thing was so unusual and disquieting that he didn't know what to reply and, satisfied, had no choice but to dismiss H.D.

Having an office at the labor service had its advantages. It made it possible to lay hands on official forms and stamps for issuing papers, passes, and the like to Italian friends who were in trouble. This was how H.D. got to know Colonel Giuseppe Montezemolo, one of the leaders of Giustizia e Libertà (a Milanese Resistance group), who was later to be shot along with three hundred thirty-five other hostages at the Ardeatine Caves at the end of March 1944. At the beginning of that year, Montezemolo told his comrades, "You can trust H.D. as one of us." Never again has H.D. been so proud of recognition.

Among other things, H.D. informed the industrialist Parodi that the SS was looking for him, and he was able to disappear successfully. To the consternation of the SS, Parodi had done something amazing in the course of carrying out an order. General Becht reported during a RuK meeting that acting on instructions, Parodi had all the requisitioned machinery from his large armaments factory in Colleferro loaded onto a long freight train for transport to Germany, but had it stopped in a tunnel and sealed-in with explosives—allegedly to protect the train from air attacks! Afterwards, a far less honorable Italian acquaintance took H.D. aside and asked him how much he wanted for having warned Parodi. H.D. told him to go to hell, and left in disgust.

At the beginning of December, the order came from Berlin to transfer the labor service to Verona before Christmas. The two central offices in Berlin had finally realized that they could expect nothing more in the way of forced labor from Rome.

On December 10, 1943, another drama was to have taken place, but unfortunately, came to nothing. Fritz Sauckel, the head of labor supply, came to Rome, for what purpose no one knew. In 1943 this man, responsible for the wretched conditions and innumerable deaths in the German labor camps, was not yet hanging on the Nuremberg gallows where he belonged (1946), but on the contrary, was still being received by his men with all honors due an arch-Nazi boss. It was a duty and a great honor for the labor service in Rome to organize an official dinner for him—and for the partisans, assisted by H.D., to organize the capture and, if need be, the killing of the criminal. H.D. contrived to be commissioned by both sides.

Santi Apostoli, the restaurant on the square of the same name, was chosen as the place of execution. Ferré had taken the job of mobilizing the partisans. He and H.D. determined the individual phases of the operation after carefully inspecting the location. The evening came and everything seemed to be going according to plan. Around 8 p.m., a light sound of brakes could be heard from the street, a car door flew open, and our hero appeared out of the darkness. Twenty invited guests lined up to shake hands, the last being H.D., since he did not exactly belong with the present company. He managed to calm his repugnance with the knowledge that the hand he was shaking would soon be that of a prisoner or a corpse.

A festive table had been set up at the end of the restaurant where there was a private dining area. It had three entrances: one in the middle, for the service, and two others completely hidden from view by screens. The partisan commandos were to gather behind the screen nearest the street, and if necessary receive instructions from H.D. in case Sauckel decided not to sit in the center.

Everyone took his seat, and H.D. felt somewhat disconcerted to find himself directly in the line of fire. His worry vanished however, at the thought of helping eliminate one of the greatest Nazi criminals or of saving the lives of many partisans by taking him prisoner.

The dinner was opulent—in the Reich, people were already starving—and the first, second, and third courses passed uneventfully except for an increase in the noise level due to alcohol. Meanwhile, H.D. had exhausted his self-imposed calm and was overcome with fear and shame. The fear was superfluous, since by now it was impossible for anything to happen; but the shame was more than justified. The partisans, to whom Ferré and H.D. had handed on a platter—so to speak—the opportunity for such an important operation, had been unable to agree among themselves on who should carry out the action.

What does all this have to do with the Kaiser's gold tableware? In the momentous days of the final quarter of 1943, occasional diversions were a necessity, and in this sense, Alfredo with his gold table service played an important role. On December 14, 1943, H.D.'s pocket diary reads: "At Alfredo's with Ferré in the evening," and on December 15th: "Departure from Rome," which H.D. was not to see again until December 1946.

March 1990

Augusta and Topolino

These were the names of two valued and indispensable automobiles—manufactured respectively by Lancia and Fiat—which were most assiduous in their aid to the chronicler. For their unquestioning obedience and participation—successful and not—in the Resistance they cannot be denied the right to the chapter-title under which the confused events of 1944-45 are gathered. Unfortunately, nowadays quantity counts more than quality, and H.D. feels he must justify the report's automotive title by the number of changes in his location and sleeping quarters during the last sixteen months of the war. To this end, he set to counting in his pocket diary and was himself surprised to find two hundred and two changes of location of at least fifty kilometers. His nocturnal accommodations were moved ninety-six times.

In the first half of 1944 H.D.'s office was transferred to Verona, once again as had been the case in Rome, as a sublease in the National Socialist labor service. His daily activities were now aimed solely at impeding everything that furthered the Nazi war effort. Later, he was often to be asked what it had been like for him after Italy's "betrayal." On April 10, 1974 he wrote:

"This amounts to a confession, since nothing would be more misleading and correspond less to the reality of those days than to put oneself in a heroic light in recounting certain episodes. First of all, we did not want to be drafted. We wanted, if possible, to eat well, to live clean and warm, even to love—all this in an uncanny atmosphere full of uncertainty and fear, combined with the hope that the chaos, which we had struggled to hold back from ourselves, would increase as much as possible, for it alone could bring about Hitler's end. So when we took certain risks upon ourselves, to protect some people or to harm others, we felt an inner satisfaction. In 1946, when a friend wanted to speak up about the summary injustice done to opponents of the Nazis in the last months of the war—which the Americans in their way were continuing by giving preferential treatment to former Nazis—I urged him not to forget how frequently and how well we had enjoyed ourselves at the time. Without thoughtless laughter we could not have survived at all. One could compare it to the hilarity that comes over many people at a funeral, even if they very much loved the deceased."

"Combing Out"

His Berlin office wanted H.D. to ensure the continuing smooth cooperation of the Italian construction companies. What he and his contacts actually did after the Italian armistice on September 8, 1943, however was to find ways to enable as many Italian workers as possible to escape and return home. He was also expected to provide forced labor, as his colonel had shown him later in that month. Making use of his military rank, this man managed to get permission to "comb out" several Italian prison camps and an English one. "Combing out" was understood to mean interrogating individual prisoners about their civilian occupation, age, and health, and when the results looked promising, separating-and shipping-out skilled workers and assistants for construction sites in Upper Silesia. Assigned as a driver and interpreter, H.D. could not avoid his superior's exploitation of his linguistic knowledge in the combing out. He consoled himself with the thought that perhaps he was a somewhat better interlocutor for those being interrogated than someone with no feeling for the injustice involved. He tried to encourage them by saying that it was better to work in your own trade than die slowly in some prison camp. He was convinced he was recommending the lesser of two evils, but felt depressed even so. He could not help thinking of the platform at Auschwitz and the order, "One to the left! One to the right!"

After combing out the Italian camps in Mantua, Modena, and Carpi—more than two hundred construction workers in all—the colonel decided to try Fiume. On September 20th, he and H.D. were flown from Venice to Fiume in a JU 52 Luftwaffe seaplane. H.D.'s pocket diary for 1943 reads, "Nice flight," but he remembers only an airsick colonel stretched out on a pile of blankets in a completely empty transport with no seats and the roaring of unmuffled motors. He found all this entertaining, especially his stricken superior. They drove directly from the port to Abazia and the hotel of the Hübner family, owners of the well-known Schönbrunn Hotel in Vienna, accompanied by the Hübner's son, who was in the service of the municipal commandant in Venice. The next day, the colonel again succeeded in combing out more than two hundred building laborers, but this time the interpreting was done by young Hübner.

Heavy rain prevented them from flying back the same day, but H.D. was again able to get satisfaction. After the combing out, on the drive back from Fiume to Abazia, the colonel trembled with fear as partisans shot at the car. He was afraid for his life the following day, too, when the over-loaded motorboat that was to carry him to the seaplane threatened to take on water. To make matters worse, the last to board the overfilled aircraft was a dead general, wrapped in a tent tarpaulin, who was laid in the aisle right next to H.D. The general arrived safely in Venice and was permitted to disembark first. Don't suppose H.D. was terribly brave himself. Only his belief that fate is programmed in advance allowed him in this case to indulge his malicious pleasure at the colonel's expense.

A Talk with Krauch

For the moment the prisoner/forced-labor operation was over. All other efforts by the colonel to inspire free Italians to take up work in Germany predictably came to nothing. This was consistent with what H.D. had explained, once again with unpardonable and inconsiderate frankness, to his highest superior on September 17, 1943, before leaving Berlin. Professor Carl Krauch, the G. B. Chem, wished to be informed about the situation in Italy after the armistice by someone who knew the country. H.D., forgetting the possible consequences for himself and his exemption from military service, gave it to him straight. Northern Italy needs Germany's help in everything. Alone, it is not a viable ally, either economically or morally. Volunteers, that is, those who were willing to work in Germany, could only be criminals looking for a place to hide or Fascists with dirt on their hands. This information obviously displeased Krauch, who broke off the conversation abruptly. When H.D. entered the ante-room of the colonel's office, after climbing four flights of stairs he heard the bewildered secretary talking on the tele-phone: "Good, I'll take care of it." She turned to H.D. "That was Krauch's secretary. The professor never wants to see Deichmann again."

The SS and the Missing Return Address

There was a Milanese lady very active in the Resistance, who was as intelligent as she was foolish. She had forgotten to give (or invent) the then obligatory return address on the envelope of a letter addressed to H.D. in Verona, announcing the arrival of a friend. The letter was opened by the SS cen-sors. Now the addressee was to be questioned. In the pres-ence of the head of the labor office, an SS officer asked him for the name of the sender of this skillfully crafted "love let-ter." Yes, he knew it—but: "Gentlemen, have you ever revealed the name of a beautiful woman who took you into her bed?" Coarse male laughter rang out. The interrogation was over.

The Dam on the Adige

Even among the Fascists in Salò, where SS Ambassador Wolff and his numerous staff held power over Mussolini, his mistress, and his impotent government (the pocket diary for January 31, 1944, reads, "All the idiots from the embassy in Rome there again"), there were a few decent people. One of them was the minister of labor, Marchiondi, who took his own life when it was all over. Marchiondi tried in many ways to prevent the forced recruitment of laborers. H.D. encountered him on several occasions, though almost exclusively as an interpreter. That was the situation on March 22nd, during a three-and-a-half-hour conference at the office in Verona of Secretary of State Landfried, head of the German military administration for Venetia. The reason for the meeting has been forgotten, but not the fact that H.D. tried to help Marchiondi by glossing over part of the translation, and that the discussion was interrupted without warning by a violent explosion. Everyone jumped up excitedly and looked at one another in bewilderment. H.D. glanced at the window just in time to see a huge wave of water rushing past and called it to the others' attention. Someone who knew something about it said a bomb must have hit the dam on the Adige above Verona, which diverted a large part of the river for irrigation. Again, it was difficult for H.D. to hide his satisfaction.

General Leyers, From Cologne!

While in Milan, H.D. was sometimes ordered to attend RuK meetings there as well. One such meeting took place on April 14-15, 1944, at Como, of which two different sorts of memories remain.

He spent the night at the Hotel Metropol, in a room whose regular occupant was temporarily absent, and discovered it belonged to Dr. Fritz terMeer. As chairman of the technical committee of I.G. Farben, terMeer had been on the seven-member central committee. No one could understand why he had been demoted in 1944 to a second-class post with the RuK in Milan. When H.D. entered the room, a city-wide blackout was in effect, and he could only reach the window on the veranda by feeling his way. Suddenly, his feet knocked against empty, overturned bottles. In the morning he found German wine bottles covering the whole floor. Evidently, terMeer, suffering from heavy depression, had had wine sent from bomb-riddled Germany to Italy—a peculiar importation one might say—to lessen his doubts of final victory.

During the meeting, General Leyers suddenly pointed to H.D., seated at the end of the table. "What does that gentleman there from the SS have to say about it?" "I'm not from the SS, General, and I have nothing to say on the matter." That evening after dinner, Leyers invited the participants over for drinks at his villa. As happens on such occasions, a lot of people got drunk, H.D. included. When his turn came to take his leave, he said, "General, many thanks for the pleasant evening, even if you did insult me deeply this afternoon. I'm not from the SS, but just from Cologne like you." The general laughed out loud, slapped his thigh like Hitler at Compiègne, and exclaimed in a strong Cologne accent to the adjutant standing beside him, "Y'hear that? He's not SS, jus' a Cologner like me!" H.D. left the room accompanied by prolonged laughter, his faith in the people of Cologne reaffirmed.

Daily Routines

In the spring of 1944, direction of the G. B. Chem's Italian office was handed over to a Nazi official from Berlin—let's call him Hardteck. H.D. was kept on as factotum (telephone operator, interpreter, provisioner, messenger, driver) since he had proved himself unfit for real, strategic war work. For him, this cover was of the greatest value, not only as protection against the military draft, but also because he had wider access to the means for his numerous actions, great and small, of support and sabotage. Specifically, he enjoyed the authority of a "Nazi commission," complete with telephone, automobile, official papers, and, his own initiative.

His friends the de Finettis lived in central Via Gesù. The official entrance to their house, which had been almost completely demolished by bombs, was located in the courtyard of No. 8. It was not generally known that one could reach No. 8 through a small courtyard at No. 6., originally intended only for servants and tradesmen. The police searched for suspects several times at No. 8. While de Finetti caused a delaying confusion with his customary sang-froid, the fugitives disappeared through No. 6, often rescued by H.D. in his official car.

Giuseppe de Finetti's brother-in-law, Hauss, an American citizen living in Italy, had joined the partisans in the Piedmont and been taken prisoner along with some of them. His family feared for his life. News came that he had been taken to the concentration camp at Bolzano. H.D. accompanied Hauss' Italian wife to the appropriate SS office in Verona and requested a visitor's permit for her. When this, predictably, was refused, he repeated his request in a letter to the head of the concentration camp and had it delivered by Signora Hauss herself, whom H.D.'s office provided with a pass for the express train to Bolzano. She did not obtain permission to speak to her husband, but food and clothing were gotten through to him. Everything turned out as expected. The only surprise was that neither the SS in Verona nor in Bolzano were interested in this strange German who intervened openly, even in writing, on behalf of an American partisan. This was one more case in a repeated pattern: unusual conduct had no place in Nazi categories of terror.

On March 30, 1944, H.D. had to drive his colonel to

Salzburg and then carry out an assignment in Munich the following day—hardly worth mentioning, were it not for the unusual entry in H.D.'s pocket diary for March 31st. "Left Salzburg 5 a.m., 25 cm. of fresh snow, Autobahn to Munich 5 hours, stuck twice, truck drove into me. 10 o'clock Munich. Agriculture Office: Colonel Weigl, Ratjen. Tail light repairs. 12:45 from Munich. 3 p.m. Stuttgart, snowstorm, windshield wiper kaput. Flat country at last, all clear to Darmstadt. Carburetor cleaned. Drove around Frankfurt, Westend completely destroyed. 6:30 p.m. at home, all well. Theo, Küsel, Meise (Frankfurt friends). Everyone talks and thinks only about air raids." How H.D. managed to drive home with the official car and obtain more than one hundred and fifty liters of gas has vanished from his memory.

The next day, H.D. visited his uncle, I.G. Farben's number one man in Frankfurt, whom the Nazis called a *Betriebsführer* ("factory leader"). His home in Westend had been bombed out, and he had makeshift quarters in Oberursel, at the spacious villa of a fellow board member, now retired, named Selck. The many residents of the house behaved as if everything were going normally. H.D. really shouldn't have been surprised when his uncle took him aside and confided to him his plans for after the war. He and his closest colleague intended to entrust H.D. with the management of sales in the Balkans. No sooner had H.D. and his wife left the house than they stopped short, aghast. "What's going on with these people? Everything happening around them they block from their minds!" Six weeks later, nothing remained of the Nazi-controlled Balkan sales territories, just as H.D. had foreseen.

In Milan, the days passed with endless errands to be run for Hardteck, two of which H.D. found amusing. In November 1944, Hardteck had gotten hold of five hundred kilos of salt which in those days was more precious than gold. H.D. was asked where one might safely store it until it could be used for ransoming some captive from the hands of the partisans? "In the I.G. Farben branch warehouse. But to ensure secrecy, every employee—around a hundred—should get a kilo of salt." Both sides agreed to this suggestion, and H.D.'s reputation among his former workmates increased immeasurably.

As late as April 1945, Hardteck had a similar worry, i.e. where could one store four hundred and fifty liters of gas? Again, H.D. communicated the willingness of the I.G. Farben branch to keep it in their warehouse, an old farmstead out in the fields of Affori, a suburb of Milan. Everyone concerned was highly satisfied—especially H.D.—when he learned three days later that a toy pistol had been used to make the timid old warehouse guard surrender it to the partisans of Giustizia e Libertà. Shortly after the war, this episode was triumphantly confessed to the director, who was not at all pleased. Such things were simply not done. He was the remotest thing from a Fascist, but rather a fine example of the confused state of mind prevalent on all sides.

A Failed Attempt

Already for several months, Hardteck had replaced H.D.—supposedly unfit and not very reliable—as office director. Nevertheless, nothing had been accomplished: no additional workers had been found for Upper Silesia. It was reported that it was still possible to round up men in Bologna, and so he decided to go there by car. The Como RuK provided him with an official vehicle and a driver. H.D. and his friends were determined to prevent the undertaking by any means and use the opportunity to kidnap or, if need be, eliminate such an arch-Nazi. As a prisoner, he would render valuable service in liberating many partisans. Instructions went out to the partisans in Bologna and the towns along the way, and confident of the outcome, the conspirators celebrated Hardteck's departure.

For two days, both sides waited anxiously for news. Suddenly, on the third day, the missing man returned to his office, without having accomplished anything, as expected. Scarcely had he entered the room when the telephone rang. H.D. heard: "Really? They wanted to take me dead or alive? The police had orders to arrest me for my protection?" He rushed over to H.D., who all the while ran hot and cold, and asked, "How is it possible that the partisans had everything: my name, the route, why I was going, the make of the car and its license plate?" After a moment's hesitation, H.D. replied, "You surely don't believe the RuK garage in Como is entirely free of partisans!" This was indeed very likely the case, but for Hardteck, the world of National Socialism was falling further out of joint. He calmed down at last, resigned. De Finetti, who had coordinated the entire operation, calmed H.D. in turn. The instructions had reached Bologna in absolute secrecy, on a sheet of notepaper torn in two, each half in the shoe of a different person. An infiltrator had, however, been discovered in their group.

An Air-raid Warning outside Bolzano

In the fall of 1944, Hardteck scored a great coup. He proudly informed the office that he had been assigned more than five hundred workers—partly volunteers, partly detainees—whom he would send to Upper Silesia in a special train within the next two days. How could this be prevented? The train would consist of regular passenger cars to be firmly bolted from the outside given the nature of the freight. H.D. immediately passed the news on to his Italian friends. A few hours later, he received instructions to assist a certain volunteer in boarding the train. This man, who would be added to the Germans' list of volunteers, was carrying a large bag full of burglar's tools.

The train was assembled at a freight yard in Milan (where the Stazione Garibaldi now stands) which did not make it any easier to outsmart the inspectors. H.D., however, managed. With much handshaking and many wishes for successful work in Germany, he helped his volunteer "friend," who had just been entrusted to him in the shadows in front of the station entrance, into his compartment. (The man could just as well have been a spy!) For safety's sake, H.D. stayed there until the well-bolted train began to move.

The next morning, a triumphant Hardteck telephoned his report to Berlin: orders carried out. While in the office, he spared no one from witnessing his superiority over his inept predecessor. His gloating, however, was premature. Disappointment came that afternoon, with the news that the train had been stopped between Trento and Bolzano because of an air-raid warning. The guards took cover, the burglar's tools went into action, and less than two hundred men arrived in Bolzano.

A Christmas Present for Krauch's Son

Christmas 1944 was drawing nearer. Even in wartime, a father is allowed the perfectly understandable desire to send his son a little gift, wherever the son might be posted. In this case the father was Professor Krauch. He is already familiar to the reader as H.D.'s highest superior. Here, too—and not only in the Holocaust at Auschwitz—he distinguished himself by a failure of the imagination. To satisfy his paternal Christmas needs, he naturally turned not to H.D. but to the colonel. He asked him to set aside his black market purchases for forty-eight hours and deliver a little package to young Captain Krauch fighting on the Apennine front to the east of Bologna. The Augusta, filled with Wehrmacht gas and driven by H.D., received orders to take the colonel, who meanwhile had become slightly unwell, from Verona to Bologna. From there, with the proper travel papers and an old soldier as escort, they drove for an hour and a half under a bright full moon through the valley, up to young Krauch's position at the front. The Augusta skillfully avoided bomb craters and horse carcasses—a white horse caressed by moonlight remains unforgotten to this day—and also eluded an enemy reconnaissance plane and its racing shadow, and finally reached its destination, where there was no shooting. The escort and H.D. discreetly stood off to one side. They had no idea what the package contained and received not even a grateful handshake.

The return journey, along a road now familiar to the Augusta, was much faster. There was enough time to hurry to the commandant's office in Bologna and make a long-distance call about essential Wehrmacht matters to Papa Krauch in Berlin. Putting three men and a car in mortal danger for the sake of a Christmas parcel was certainly worthwhile. The officers' quarters sheltered the travelers, undisturbed by air-raid warnings.

The Berlin Freight Car

The pocket diary for December 2, 1944, reads, "Milan: Berlin freight car left"—left, that is, for the G.B. Chem's office in Berlin. It would be a mistake to think this railroad car contained valuable chemicals crucial for the war effort. The contents were exclusively black-market goods: cognac, wine, oil, flour, sugar, coffee, shoes, and even men's and women's underwear. On December 7, 1944, the colonel was presented with a watch by some Italian construction companies, so he could "forget" about elusive construction workers.

As so often before, with the help of his pocket diary, H.D. remembers exactly what happened in the days that followed. There were intense preparations for the colonel's departure. He wanted to arrive in Berlin together with the freight car—the real fruit of his work in Italy—to preside over the inequitable distribution of riches among his colleagues. He was anxious to leave. The honeymoon was over. The colonel, his secretary, and another three hundred kilos of black-market goods were packed into the Augusta. It was a sturdy car. Nevertheless, the pocket diary reads: "December 8: distributor broke after Arco, towed to Trento . . . on three legs over terrible road to Bressanone. December 9: 7 a.m., garage: new spark plugs, tire chains. 9:45, leave Bressanone, air alarm until 1:30 p.m. 2:10 p.m., leave Innsbruck station."

Krauch's Recommendation to Kesselring

The Augusta almost forgot one last crime. The previous day, the colonel was driven to Arco, on the northern tip of Lake Garda. There, in a military hospital, Field Marshal Kesselring was recovering from injuries suffered in an automobile accident. The colonel handed him a letter—which H.D. had read. Professor Krauch (before his fit of amnesia five months later) was requesting that the Wehrmacht during its retreat skirmishes pick up all ablebodied men in central and northern Italy and send them to Upper Silesia as slave laborers. Kesselring turned down the proposal on military grounds.

A General on the Brenner Road

The pocket diary entry "leave Innsbruck" referred only to the colonel's train. Immediately afterward H.D., enjoying his renewed privacy, patted the Augusta affectionately. "Take me straight to Verona. Friends are expecting me there."

But things didn't go as smoothly as he had hoped. Though lightened of its load, the Augusta needed eight hours to complete the journey. H.D.'s precious solitude was ended when an SS officer was taken on at the Brenner Pass. At one of the steep stretches of road just before Bressanone, an army truck with a trailer blocked the way in both directions, its wheels stuck fast in a bomb crater. In the middle of the line of vehicles sat a general, growling ineffectually in his open car. The situation seemed hopeless . . . but not for H.D. He urged the general to take command: all the drivers, with him in front as a good example, should heave the truck out of the hole together. After some hesitation—a general cannot allow himself to take orders from a civilian—the general performed his duty. The road was open again in a relatively short time.

Taking advantage of his fellow-countrymen's slow headway, H.D. now tried to pass the other vehicles and put himself at the head of the column. The general jumped out of his car, tore open the Augusta's door, and screamed his protest into H.D.'s ear, while slamming the door repeatedly with violence. "Stop that at once, or I'll report you for wanton destruction of Wehrmacht property!" H.D. shouted back, quite spontaneously, without figuring the odds for a German general's cringing when properly yelled at. But that is what happened. The Augusta was allowed to drive on, with a formerly talkative SS passenger who now held a respectful silence. In Bolzano, with the deepest gratitude and a Heil Hitler, he left the Augusta and its "important" driver to enjoy their time alone.

Radio London Accompanies an SS Interrogation

A friend, the building contractor Colombo, was suspected of supporting the partisans of his native village, Monticelli on the Po—this suspicion was well-founded. He was summoned to a command post in the foothills of the Apennines by the Italian SS (yes, such a thing existed, pathetic as it was). H.D. had to protect Colombo, "a fellow-fighter for the final victory, completely loyal to the Germans." For this purpose, two older German soldiers in Milan were recruited for the expedition. The group reached its destination toward 11 p.m., on February 1, 1945, after an excellent supper at Colombo's mother's house. The accusations were just as primitive as the interrogators and readily demolished by H.D.'s German authority. But the report, which was typed with one finger, took forever. To pass the time, H.D. turned on a decrepit radio receiver, and lo and behold! Radio London's German broadcast provided some diversion. Only after a good while did the German soldiers notice it. H.D.—with some difficulty—convinced them it was a mistake.

Red-and-gold Braid

On April 25, 1945 in Milan, the last German general H.D. laid eyes on, was showing-off his red-and-gold braid. It was a historic day for Italy, but only partly so for the Germans, who had another ten days to go before their total surrender. The name of the general—as Ernst Nolte would wish—has faded from memory after so many years. Suffice it to say, he had been the German commandant of Milan up until that day. A few important events, however, preceded H.D.'s sight of him. Hence another plea for the reader's patience.

Fearing an imminent battle for Milan, most Germans, including Hardteck and his gang, had abandoned the city the previous evening and headed for Trentino-Alto Adige in the southern Tirol. The end of German command dismayed others who were about to pull out, though they were still seeking the protection of the Wehrmacht in the Alps. H.D.'s decision to stay in Milan was registered with only a shake of the head in place of any heartfelt objection. Fear for their own skins played a role in this, for one less man and his baggage increased the vehicular space for stolen goods and the chances for the eager fugitives to get away. At this time Hardteck requisitioned the Milan house of H.D.'s friends the Ferrés, expressly to protect it from other greedy coveters. This, however, did not prevent him from taking everything useful and cramming it into two cars he had sequestered for himself. We will let him go his way. H.D. never saw him again.

The entry in the pocket diary for April 25, 1945, reads, "3 p.m., Via Gesù, after final trip with Augusta (to de Finnetti's) . . . mobilization with Topolino." H.D. was received at Via Gesù by Beppi Signorelli, one of the most active members of Giustizia e Libertà, who said, "Tonight, the partisans will drive the Germans out of the city. I've got to mobilize the workers in the San Siro district. Drive me there!" It occurred to no one, least of all H.D., that this was not without danger for an "accursed" German . . . so away they went.

After driving some twenty minutes through the empty city, the Topolino came to a large many-storied housing complex. Beppi jumped out and vanished without giving H.D. any instructions. The spring sun was shining warmly and invitingly: what lay ahead was bound to turn out well. H.D. relaxed and gave in to his desire to get out of the car and sit on the hood.

After a few minutes, he found himself surrounded by a cluster of curious people. "But you're German, right?" one of them said at last, voicing the general perplexity. H.D. nodded, smiling a little uncertainly. He was beginning to grasp that he was in a situation only his closest confidants could understand. The bystanders were obviously asking themselves: "What's this German doing here with a German military car, in a quarter of the city held by partisans? What'll we do with him? Take him prisoner? Beat him? At any rate, let's take his car." For a while nothing happened. They talked back and forth in dialect. H.D. told the truth. He was helping to mobilize the partisans. But this only increased their amazement and suspicion. Both sides, thank God, were hesitant. Then

Beppi Signorelli came running out of a doorway toward the little crowd, waving in a conciliatory way from afar. By now he too had realized that the situation could be dangerous for H.D. He stepped into the middle of the circle and explained gravely that this man here—pointing to H.D.—had been a trusted friend of theirs for a long time. This was not the first time he had helped us. Great relief on all sides, with shoulder-clapping, handshakes, and good-luck wishes. The Topolino drove off amid cheers.

Beppi clearly did not want to put H.D. in danger again. He asked to be dropped off in another district and then sent him home.

Before H.D. returned to the safekeeping of his friends at Via Gesù, an important matter had to be arranged: the restitution of the Topolino to its legitimate owners. How would he manage that? His route from the outskirts to the center of the city led through Via Sardegna, where the customs police had taken up quarters in a large school building. They had a reputation for unbending anti-Fascism, and H.D. decided on the spot to hand over the car to these representatives of the Italian state. He entered through the big front gate and had to clear his throat loudly several times before a door finally opened at the end of a long corridor.

The weary voice of a very young soldier asked, "What do you want?" Here peace and tranquillity reigned. Nothing could be felt of the tensions outside.

"I want to return a car."

"You want to what? Return a car? What kind of car? Why?"

"A car the Germans appropriated from the Italian state. The war's over now, and the car has to be returned to its owners."

"Just a moment, I'll have to call the lieutenant." After a while, a lieutenant appeared, clearly just as baffled. The same questions, the same answers.

"Give me a receipt and I'll be satisfied," said H.D. "I'll leave right away." The lieutenant wrote laboriously on a scrap of paper, pausing again and again in astonishment that he had taken possession of a Topolino from Signor So-and-so. Highly satisfied, H.D. went out into the street, which without his friend the Topolino seemed even emptier than before.

It was a long way back from there, almost an hour on foot. The sun was shining, the war was ending, even though no one quite knew how it would work itself out. It was obviously over in Milan. The mobilization of the outskirts had probably been unnecessary. All this H.D. sensed with a jubilation tempered with fear as he walked on. He was almost at his destination when he reached the intersection of Via Manzoni and Via Monte Napoleone, a short distance from Via Gesù, where for ages the Hotel de la Ville had watched over the corner. There, in 1901, Verdi had died and straw had been spread on the surrounding pavement so that the clumping of horses' hoofs would not disturb the invalid composer. The absolute stillness of this April 25th made H.D. muse that straw was superfluous now. Even the big electric clock, which adorned the corner of the hotel like a Chinese lantern, had stopped at 1:28 p.m. Something decisive must have happened.

Then, suddenly, came the sound of approaching motor vehicles. How? From where? To H.D.'s great surprise, a small Wehrmacht contingent of four cars appeared, traveling slowly, almost ceremoniously, down Via Manzoni from Piazza Cavour. In the lead was a kind of jeep mounted with four machine guns turned threateningly toward the houses.

Following it was a huge open Horch such as German bigwigs normally used, and in it glittered the red-and-gold braid
of a general, the commandant of Milan. He sat there erect
and silent. No doubt he missed the applause—or even perhaps the hostile fear—of curious crowds lining the streets.
The only available target was H.D., his presence inexplicable
to the soldiers. Now even he was afraid. He had considered
it far too late in the game to be shot. He pressed himself
against the wall of the hotel, which offered him no cover at
all, and held his breath. Then the small column, with two
more jeeps bristling with weapons, passed by. H.D. immediately recovered from his fright. What he had seen would
remain fixed in his memory as one of the most sublime
moments in his life.

Some minutes later, at Via Gesù, the strange, final
appearance of the Wehrmacht was explained. In the Palazzo
dei Giornali in Piazza Cavour, the general had just signed the
surrender of the German occupation force, which guaranteed
safe return to his "compound" (as the Americans in Frankfurt later called it) on Piazzale Brescia, there to give himself
up not to the partisans, but to the approaching Allies.

April 1990

THE RUBBER THIMBLE

In Frankfurt on January 2, 1931, the chronicler, H.D., was handed a rubber thimble, the I.G. Farben "emblem" for apprentices. He remembers his enthusiasm instantly fading only to be replaced with doubts as to whether he had, after all, chosen the wrong profession. Then again, had he ever really had a choice? By 1930 things were going pretty badly for Germany—industrial production had sunk to half of what it had been in 1929 and six million people were unemployed. Prospects for earning a living in a profession related to the law were next to nil, and he would have had to apprentice himself without pay for a few years. By this point, H.D. could no longer rely on prolonged financial support from home.

A few weeks before starting work in Frankfurt, he had handed in his dissertation in Bonn—*State Supervision of National Foundations*. It had led to a clash between a civil law professor of whom he was not particularly fond and H.D.'s dissertation advisor, a constitutional law specialist who was primarily interested in dissertations dealing with topics in his own field of specialization. H.D. did not particularly relish the subject of his dissertation, but he enjoyed stepping into the arena in support of his director against the other professor.

It was a painful step, leaving the university library to

face a large pile of invoices that H.D. had to arrange, with the help of the rubber thimble, into an apparently incomprehensible system. No one told him where the invoices came from, what they had been for, or what their fate would be after he had finished sorting them. He was told that the customer books of each division of I.G. Farben had to be maintained in the Frankfurt office. There was also a *special* bookkeeping branch, and H.D. spent nine months in both offices without learning a thing about bookkeeping: no one paid any attention to the apprentices. In 1931, it seemed to be enough for I.G. Farben that he had been integrated into its hierarchy—and that for a monthly pittance of forty reichsmarks!

All that H.D. remembers of those first months of his so-called apprenticeship was that he met a fellow sufferer. He, too, was a university man who had worked at Bayer in Leverkusen, where he had been offered the option of either resigning or accepting a transfer to central bookkeeping in Frankfurt. Since it was practically impossible to find work elsewhere in 1931 he sat there just as unhappily as H.D. In the sea of bookkeeping stations, the two of them managed to secure workspaces opposite each other. They found that the middle drawers of their desks were connected in such a way that if one kicked one's own drawer, the opposite one would pop open and poke the person facing in the stomach. Both did this quite often to cheer each other up.

How did one finagle extra days off, when vacations were limited to fourteen days? In 1931, H.D. managed to get an additional two weeks off in order to defend his dissertation. Having learned this trick, the following year he asked for four weeks to further his knowledge of English in Britain. As he already had a relatively good command of English, he spent the four weeks which were granted in Austria at the Grundlsee with his friends the Schwarzwalds. In Bad Aussee he quickly ducked into a side street when he saw the brother of his department manager! (In 1936, on returning from France, he maintained that he had yet to take his vacation, and so managed once more to land himself a four week leave.)

H.D. remembers his apprenticeship as the drabbest and emptiest period of his life. He was obsessed by the idea of switching to a civil service job. On April 16, 1932, Genia Schwarzwald wrote to him: "When it comes to your career, I am a bit of a coward. Not that I think much of I.G. Farben— you've painted quite a clear picture. But I'm not sure I really trust the civil service. How can I counsel you to let go of the I.G. Farben plank in the torrential river of our times, when I have nothing concrete to suggest?"

In December 1932, the directors of I.G. Farben decided to have all apprentices take a newfangled American intelligence test. The apprentices were given an automatic calculation board which moved back and forth horizontally adding rows of ten times ten two-digit numbers arranged next to each other. H.D. completed the first column quickly and easily. When he got to the second row he was beginning to find the constriction unbearable, managing to do fewer and fewer additions until, furious, he crossed out the whole final row. There was also an essay the apprentices had to write on one of three possible subjects. H.D. chose "Frankfurt," declaring it to be a horrendous city, made bearable only by the presence of the Jews. The examiners gave him high marks, grading him as "unusual." So it must have been a good test after all!

Sitting at the desk next to H.D. was a registrar with a golden Nazi emblem on his lapel. During tea breaks, he strove to fill the gaps in his intelligence by reading the *Völkischer Beobachter*, the Nazi paper. H.D. looked over the registrar's shoulder and, pointing at a picture of Hitler, said, "I think it's pretty obvious that a man with such a face could never become the chancellor of Germany." That was two months before the Nazis came to power. Shortly thereafter, on January 1, 1933, H.D. was moved to a different department and given a salary of a hundred and ninety reichsmarks. After the Nazis took over on January 30, 1933, he ran into the now trium-phant registrar in a corridor.

"Well, what do you have to say now?" the registrar asked.

"One can't always be right!" H.D. answered, which didn't seem to go over too well. A bitter smile, a quick "Heil Hitler!" and they never met again.

Shortly before this incident, H.D. had had the opportu-nity to confirm his opinion of Hitler's physiognomy at close quarters. At the beginning of December 1932, he had gone to Berlin for the weekend to see Genia Schwarzwald (it was to be her last visit to Germany). As the train was about to leave the Magdeburg Station, H.D. was sitting in the dining car having a sandwich, when his meal was rudely interrupted by the Horst Wessel Song and loud shouts of "Heil Hitler!" on the platform. After a few seconds, a typically Prussian aide-de-camp appeared, looked about the dining car, and took a seat facing the sufficiently-blond H.D. Shortly thereafter, Hitler himself appeared, escorted by more aides-de-camp, and took a seat by the window facing H.D. H.D. was not even curious, as he usually would be. He was disgusted. Hitler was dirty, his suit covered with oily stains, the collar and cuffs of his shirt grimy. Let's not mention his hands. After they had ordered food, Hitler turned to his companions and said: "That girl in the row in front of me was pretty, wasn't she? But all anyone ever wants from me is talk, talk, talk, and more talk!" Then they ate. Hitler eating! A good reason to duck and run. So H.D. paid his check and left instead of using the opportunity to have a chat with Hitler. H.D. couldn't and wouldn't believe that only two months later this grubby little man was to become the German chancellor. And he seemed in no way fascinating, as so many people declared later on. Hitler was simply disgusting.

After the bleak first two years of apprenticeship, things got better. In March of 1933, H.D. was sent, like all other apprentices, to Höchst for one-and-a-half months to study dyeing. That is, he was taught hands-on in the actual laboratory the different methods of dyeing and printing textiles with organic dyes. H.D. enjoyed working with the substances to which he would be dedicating his professional life, so he requested authorization for an additional six weeks' learning period. The request was granted. As a happy memento of these three months, he kept for many years the samples that he himself had produced.

Working in the dye laboratories at Höchst also had a very different advantage: in the laboratories you were both cut off and hidden from the horrendous Nazi occurrences of the first six months of 1933. No one cornered you into taking a political stance. It is unthinkable what might have happened had H.D. been in daily contact with the Nazi enthusiasts at the I.G. Farben offices.

Contrary to the chronicler's initial resolution to keep every object the basic focal point of each story, the rubber thimble at this point falls away, but won't disappear as revisionist historian Ernst Nolte would recommend. Before we abandon it completely, the chronicler would like to touch on what it was that allowed him to survive those first two years at I.G. Farben in one piece. H.D. cut his day into two strict sections: the almost invariably tedious eight working hours that ended at 5 p.m., and the single-minded quest for enjoyment in the remaining sixteen hours.

He found superb hospitality at his uncle's house, even if the uncle, who was Number One at I.G. Farben and had paved the way for H.D.'s career there, never questioned the abominable neglect of the "rubber thimbles." For two years, H.D. managed to keep the family connection a secret. On one hand, he did not want to be accused of profiting from his family connection, and on the other, he was ashamed of his uncle's failure—to the detriment of the firm—to give apprentices useful training. The high point of his uncle's hospitality was the frequent meals—with a cousin of his who was more than ten years his junior—on the secluded second floor of the house. H.D. spent weekends in Heidelberg with his girlfriend whom he had been dating since he had been a student in Bonn.

His most important friendship at the time was with Hanna Bekker von Rath. She was the daughter of a cousin of H.D.'s grandfather. Despite the age difference, they took to each other right from the start. He visited her almost every week in Hofheim, and could thus witness her first steps in collecting the art that today hangs in the Wiesbadener Museum. He came to know German Expressionism well. One day, he managed to convince Hanna that a hands-on woman like her had to learn how to drive a car and also suggested they share one. (A friend later said that H.D.'s methods as a driving instructor could jeopardize even the sturdiest friendship.) Hanna would drive the car on weekdays, H.D. on weekends. There is a photograph of Hanna sitting under the Acropolis in their co-owned two-cylinder Tatra.

After his period in the dye laboratory in Höchst, H.D. was sent for six months to Leipzig, to I.G. Farben's largest sales office in Germany. He accompanied the sales representatives on their visits to clients and learned "how things were done." These six months, plus two more months in a dye factory in Kulmbach, brought him into open contact with everyday Nazi life. It wasn't as bad as he had expected, but perhaps only because up to that point relatively few people had come face to face with Nazi terror, which, in the years 1933-34, was still carefully hidden. Unlike later, after Hindenburg's death, and after the total devastation of the conservatives. The workers at the dye factory were not yet shouting "Heil Hitler!" as a greeting, but were happy to be employed.

H.D. returned to Frankfurt and I.G. Farben, where he was to prepare himself in the division responsible for France for a year's training in that country. But the head of the department turned him down, claiming that it was doubtful that H.D. would be issued a work permit for Paris, and, in any case, the department could not carry H.D.'s salary of two hundred and twenty reichsmarks per month. H.D. was suspicious, and checked. He found that this division had made a clean profit of 1.1 million reichsmarks in 1933. So, until his papers for France were ready, H.D. moved to the central office from which international dye cartels were administered. Fate smiled upon him. A Nazi working in the department was dismissed for fraud and, overnight, H.D. was given his position. In the three months before he left for France, he learned more than he had in the previous twenty-seven as an apprentice.

May 1990

The Elevator

March 25, 1944. The chronicler was on his way out of the house at Corso Littorio 5, in Milan—today Corso Matteotti. He took the elevator down from the fifth floor, and, as the door opened in the lobby, came face to face with a woman who was waiting impatiently. She was beautiful and extremely well groomed—a rare sight in those days. If her face hadn't been so angry and aristocratic, her dark hair, blue eyes, and pale complexion could have made her pass for a fully mature Snow White. The building housed the offices of the steelworks that belonged to her husband, and since their home had been bombed, she had found a most elegant refuge on the sixth floor.

Up to that day, she had never spoken a word to any of the Germans stationed in the building. But in a fit of anger, she now turned to H.D. and shouted: "Don't you know that it's against the law to ride the elevators down? There's a war going on—we must save electricity!"

H.D. never liked being reprimanded, especially in matters of war and, startled for a moment, he looked at her and said:

"What did you have for lunch today?"

"How dare you ask me such a question!" she flung back at him with as much indignation as surprise.

"It's quite simple: more likely than not, you bought food on the black market—in other words illegally—which is perfectly fine with me. Everyone breaks the rules. You eat, I ride down on elevators. Good day, Madam!"

She stood there speechless, and he escaped as fast as he could to hide his embarrassment at his own response.

In the summer of 1945, he finally had the opportunity to offer his apologies to the beautiful woman . . . and to see her again. He asked a mutual friend, who was well known in Milan society as an anti-Fascist, to introduce him, and he introduced himself, handing her a large bouquet of marguerites. The meeting was a disappointment. The beautiful woman received him cordially—somewhat too cordially to allow hopes of a more intimate nature. She was also not prepared to make light of their previous meeting . . . nor was she quite as beautiful as she had been.

September 1990

THE LIFEBED

The chronicler is proud of this object—and the new term he has coined for it. The concept comes from "lifeboat;" as both objects have it in common that they save lives. But while saving lives is a lifeboat's sole task, a bed usually saves them only after its other duties have been successfully performed. As we shall soon see this was the case in this story too.

The war had just ended, and in the winter of 1945-46 Germany's bombed-out cities had summoned everyone back to try and settle into the rubble as best they could. This was also true of the District Court in Frankfurt on the Zeil Concourse. Its official address was on a remote side street, but one could only get there by following a path decorated with countless arrows, winding through the ruins of the buildings that had stood along the Zeil. The undamaged part of the stairs inside the building led up to the second floor, where a notice hung of the divorce hearing to which H.D. had been summoned as a witness. It was bitter cold in the hall, so he knocked on the door. "Yes, come in, come in! According to the rules, one must wait outside until summoned, but it's much too cold for that!" the judge called out, and H.D. went inside and sat down.

The petitioner was about H.D.'s age and a close relative. She had asked him to testify in court about her husband's adulterous behavior in Italy during the final year of the war, and had made him swear that on no account was he to digress into political territory. Until the end of the war, her husband had been a Nazi consul in SS uniform in Turin, and she did not want the divorce to hinge on those grounds, but rather on the fact that he was a complete bastard. It had been common knowledge throughout his area of jurisdiction in northern Italy that he was having an affair with a beautiful woman from Turin's aristocratic circles. The affair was of course enough grounds for divorce.

After the customary legal formalities, H.D. was called to the witness stand.

"Your profession?"

"Unemployed."

"How can you offer evidence in favor of the petitioner?"

"Well, I was an official of the German Administration in Milan at the same time that the petitioner's husband was the consul for Nazi Germany in Turin."

The petitioner went white when she heard "Nazi Germany," and whiter still as H.D. continued:

"Under different circumstances, it might have been arguable that his extramarital affair was a mere rumor. In this case, however, the decisive factor is that whenever I or my friends from the Italian Resistance wanted to save someone from the SS or other Nazi persecutors, all we had to do was turn to the consul's girlfriend in Turin for help. And before you knew it, salvation came from her bed, where she invariably interceded with the consul on behalf of our men. No one had the slightest doubt as to the nature of the methods used!"

"I don't have the slightest doubt either," the judge said. "The witness may leave the stand."

H.D. rose, sought out the thankful eyes of the once

more rosy-cheeked petitioner, and, amused, left the wrecked courthouse.

Funny how this bed, he smiled to himself, with the same simple method, brought salvation to such different people: life to the partisans, freedom to the consul's wife.

October 1990

The Suitcase

Objects and subjects, in order of their appearance:
> —the suitcase
> —its colonel
> —his Nazi escort
> —the Italian building contractors
> —a taxi driver
> —Bernini's stairs
> —two Swiss papal guards*
> —two halberds
> —a welcoming priest*
> —Raphael**
> —Pope Pius XII
> —H.D., the chronicler*

It was a time when suitcases were subjects and the people attached to them objects—October 1943. (In May, the soldiers of the Axis were driven out of North Africa. The Allies landed in Sicily in June, and Mussolini was apprehended. At the end of September, the Allies landed at Salerno and Mussolini, now Hitler's straw man, returned as *Il Duce* of

---

*Presumably still alive.
**The only immortal one.

the Social Republic of Salò. All this, while the Russians were advancing irresistibly in the east). What would things have come to if suitcases had not so generously assisted in the transport of black-market goods? That in our case the subject (the suitcase) was carried in the end by the object (the colonel) does not disrupt the hierarchy.

Popes are carried in sedan chairs. Sedan chairs are carried in turn by bearers. So here we have more than one subject. Only the pope always remains an object. Here this object takes the form of a conduit for the transmission of an error that is most peculiar, originating as it does with the head of Christendom. The error lies in the belief that one can master Evil with the help of a greater evil. Even then, people wondered whether this conduit of errors ever stopped to consider what would have become of him if he had to face the victorious greater evil—with whom he had cast his lot—alone. (For those still in the dark, or who insist on remaining so: the evils were none other than Stalin and Hitler.)

Now to the suitcase. It may have come originally from Zehlendorf or Neukölln or some other bombed-out quarter in Berlin—it's not important. What is important is that its owner had the face of a German colonel. This man had landed in Rome, accompanying the suitcase, along with an arch-Nazi from his office who was to replace H.D. six months later. His intention was to procure additional construction workers for himself, or rather, for his superior, the quote-unquote "General Plenipotentiary for Special Questions of Chemical Production." No, not even for him, but for the large chemical factory sites in Upper Silesia that he controlled. In March 1942, about eight thousand such workers materialized as the fruit of a contract with the Fascist building contractors association in Rome. Thousands more were to follow, as the fruit of the enslavement of Italy after September 8, 1943. In 1942, the Italian building contractors, German sympathizers, were simply greedy for profit. A year and a half later, they were anxious only not to be accused—after the expected German defeat—of aiding and abetting Nazi crimes.

The Italian building contractors conferred with H.D. How could they send the colonel back to Berlin satisfied, without making any concessions? "Let's fill his suitcase with black-market goods," they suggested. "And if possible, get him a private audience with the pope." H.D. was equally surprised and charmed by the idea. He trusted in the helplessness of his fellow-countrymen when faced with anything impromptu. He was sure that something as extraordinary as a papal hand-shake would make the colonel forget everything else and depart, content with empty promises. Nevertheless, there were doubts about the feasibility of the scheme.

When two days later H.D. learned that the pope actually expected them for a private audience (a reception for twenty people where he says a few words to each) sabotaging the purpose of the colonel's visit became almost a matter of indifference. He was possessed by the idea that he could use this unique opportunity to tell the pope what his aunt, the wife of the German ambassador to the Holy See, had been unwilling to say six months earlier: that all Christendom was expecting the pope, as guardian of the Ten Commandments, to excommunicate Hitler at last. Everyone who urged it, whether on religious or strictly political grounds, was convinced that unmasking this criminal would shorten the war and save millions of people from annihilation.

These preliminary remarks serve to put the suitcase in its German context. A taxi was called on the morning of October 17, 1943. There were only a few of them, and one never knew which was older, the driver or the car. Among the four passengers however, the suitcase was undoubtedly the oldest. It was a physical and mental presence, taking up a good deal of room in the taxi as well as in the colonel's head. "To the Vatican, audience entrance, please." One could count on an old taxi driver to know where to go. Without hesitation, he drove to the great entryway where the Bernini columns begin their path around Piazzo San Pietro, almost directly under the window from where the pope customarily shows himself and blesses the crowds.

The guests were received by a splendid, colorfully uniformed Swiss Guard, friendly, but with a stern expression. Finding the invitation in order, he gestured with his halberd toward the ascending stairs.

Obeying the guard, the three guests, without the suitcase, mounted one of the world's most beautiful and impressive stairways. Thanks to its very low, deep steps, this stairway, a good five meters wide, can be climbed even on horseback, not to mention by sedan chair. H.D. was lost in admiration, and also thinking over his planned conversation with the pope, when suddenly, halfway up, the colonel turned to him and whispered in agitation: "For God's sake, my suitcase! I left it in the taxi!"

"What of it? You know the taxi's going to pick us up, no doubt with the suitcase."

The colonel sighed deeply, knowing exactly how things go in this wicked world. He was brooding and anxious, unable to be comforted. "You know how dishonest the Italians are. The taxi certainly won't come back."

H.D. tried inviting him to admire the stairway, but could not appease the colonel, devastated by the recent turn of events. Meanwhile, after conquering the last of the steps, they came to a second guard, just as colorful as the first and likewise armed with a halberd. By then, H.D.'s last and rather impatient remark was just beginning to irritate the colonel: the suitcase was anything but attractive and certainly no temptation for a Roman taxi driver. But there was no time to elaborate. At a signal from the guard, a priest in a simple black frock stepped out of a breathtakingly frescoed hallway. After a brief greeting, friendly but reserved, he gave them to understand that he was to escort them to the audience chamber. A seemingly endless tour took them through room after room of unforgettably rich colors. No doubt the dramatic events depicted in Raphael's frescoes make everything loom large in H.D.'s memory. He was so dazzled by it all that he nearly missed the nod from the priest telling them to stop.

They were on the side of the hall opposite the stairs. A great folding door on their right opened, and out stepped the fascinating, tall figure of Pius XII in full splendor, followed by a flock of cardinals and other dignitaries. He seemed to be absorbed in his own thoughts and, not deigning to glance at anyone, hurried past his visitors. It would have been easy to reach out and touch him. Then, at the far end of the wide corridor, another folding door opened, swallowing up him and his companions. The whole thing took less than a half-minute, but it was enough to intimidate H.D. and make him doubt whether his plan could be realized. They were told that the pope had just returned from a beatification in the Sistine Chapel and would hold his audience shortly.

A few more steps, and they found themselves in the audience chamber, not much larger than necessary to accommodate four times five people standing in square formation. There were already seventeen others waiting, all in German uniforms. Finding out which contractors had arranged the audience for these people was prevented by further concerns about the troubling suitcase and the sight of the pope, who had just swept past.

After standing around silently for fifteen minutes, yet another door opened, and Pius XII entered, now in his white workaday habit. The square unfolded and received him into its center. He greeted the company with a brief, entirely forgettable speech, ending it with a papal blessing. At once, he began his rounds, asking each and every one if he were behaving well—the answer invariably: "yes"—offered his ring to be kissed, and had an assistant distribute small silver medals. Pius XII reached H.D. almost last. The chronicler was waiting between the colonel and his Nazi escort but had enough time to realize that only German was being spoken. Thus it would be impossible to switch over into Italian, and, at that, H.D. lost his courage. The by now customary question was put to him. He made no reply. The pope rewarded him with a surprised glance, and then, after a slight hesitation, turned to the next in line. H.D. was in complete despair, holding himself now responsible for all the horrors that would continue to spread unchecked.

In another few minutes, Pius XII completed his rounds and vanished, unmoved.

H.D. would probably not have been able to pull himself together so quickly were it not for the suitcase. Scarcely had they left the audience chamber when the colonel began to raise a clamor again. They descended the magnificent stairway with H.D. unable to get in a word of reply. And outside at the entryway—no taxi! But before the colonel could crow "You see!" H.D. caught sight of it at a distance, bumping toward them across the cobbled square. As it neared, the suitcase could also be seen, in a state of perfect contentment. To the "You see!" of the chronicler our object made no reply, unfazed by the fact a German colonel in October 1943, amid bombs, war crimes, and even the attentions of the pope, should have only the fate of a suitcase on his mind.

H.D. was reminded again of Pius XII, the suitcase, and the colonel in the summer of 1952, when he took the *Rules for Confession* from the door of the cathedral of Spoleto and read:

1) Absolution cannot be granted to Catholics who are members of groups or parties condemned by the Church.

2) The confessor can only grant absolution to a socialist or a communist if he promises to return or destroy his party membership card.

Spoleto, June 6, 1952
The Church Council

Look at that, thought H.D. to himself. Renouncing the fight against the greater evil hasn't made the Church at all more Christian . . .

January 1991

RAILROAD TRACKS

There were various contestants for the title of this piece: two stations, railroad tracks, and fear. The stations had no platforms nor anyplace for people to get on or off a train. Although these three title choices were not actually in any way connected, they played a resoundingly important role in H.D.'s life. "Fear" came from looking at the tracks; a fear that H.D. had only recently overcome. But in May 1991, railroad tracks—tracks leading from Katowice to Wroclaw—became the main point of interest for the chronicler.

Four days before, H.D. and Luisa had flown to Krakow. Poland had just opened its borders, a fact that still confused the man at passport control, who spent almost as much time looking for nonexistent visas as it had taken Alitalia to fly from Rome. This, however, did not spoil the charming reception that H.D. and Luisa were given by two extraordinarily helpful Italian organizers of the trip or the punctual beginning of the extensive itinerary of the next few days. This itinerary began with the international *Triennale di Grafica*. There wasn't much to see, but the exhibition did give one a sense of the intensity and friendliness of the intellectual life of this town, cut off from the West for so many years. It was, however, all the more frustrating not to be able to speak with anyone and having to make do with silently taking in one's surroundings. It was tough overcoming the language barrier, and for the entire week he spent in Poland, H.D. didn't quite manage to do it. As the days passed, he wondered more and more how the people of East and West could get closer to each other despite this language barrier.

Krakow is a feast for the eyes. This venerable, lively town is full of relics from all eras. Besides its incredible historic legacy, what is most noticeable is that the old part of town has larger and straighter streets than any other equally ancient town. The many stately villas remind one of Austria—and why should the Habsburgs not have left their fingerprints here too? Something else is immediately striking: The town survived the war unscathed. No German should forget however, that from 1939 to 1944 Krakow was used as a base from which to annihilate the upper crust of Polish society. H.D. pondered this as he stood on the Wawel, the hill with its mighty cathedral and its labyrinthine castle from which all of Poland's kings reigned. So did Hans Frank, the Nazi governor-general for five years. He was condemned to death at the Nurenberg trials.

If one thinks about what the Germans and the Russians have done to Poland, it is understandable why after 1945 so few people tried to learn the malefactors' languages. Here, it is like a breath of fresh air when you find someone who speaks at least a little English. On the second day of the journey, H.D. and his companions were riding in a cab from the outskirts of town to the center when the cab driver, noticing that his passengers were Italian, launched-in on an effervescent speech (in English), the gist of which was that everything in the city was of Italian origin. This could not be left unchallenged. A protracted exchange culminated with the cab driver's proposal to take them to Auschwitz two days later for $45.

Their present ride into the city was to be free of charge.

They hadn't planned to go to Auschwitz; it hadn't even crossed H.D.'s mind. But suddenly it became the focal point of the whole journey—to see the place, after forty-seven years, which he had visited ten times—I.G. Farben had had its construction site there—between March 1942 and November 1944. In July 1943, when the murders had reached a high point and everyone was talking about them at the construction site, H.D. realized that the horrendous atrocities of the Nazi regime would end only with the loss of the war. From that point on, he had decided to do his best to help bring this about.

With every kilometer of the beautiful, hilly landscape the travelers grew more restless with anticipation. H.D. remembered only a few details from the past, and these he wanted to see again at all cost. The village of Auschwitz had in the meantime turned into a town of 30,000 inhabitants, and the Buna synthetic rubber factory had turned into a sprawling chemical concern.

H.D. wanted to see the train station first. As luck would have it, there was still a small part of the old stable-like barracks there, waiting to be torn down. But even in the new station building there seemed to be no provision for a platform. H.D. left the station rather disappointed. It stood, and still stands, as an important symbol in his life.

Then H.D. and his helpful cab driver drove around looking for the two hills that were near the old I.G. Farben site. On one of them the barracks had stood for the Italian construction companies with their three thousand workers H.D. had to care for. From this site one had a bird's-eye view of the gigantic I.G. Farben works, and further down, about four kilometers away, the smoking crematoria of Birkenau. One could still see traces of the old excavations of the I.G. Farben site, where the new chemical plant was now standing, but there were no signs left of the old guesthouse, which had stood nearby on the second hill.

Thus ended the revisiting of old haunts, and H.D. and his party drove to the Auschwitz Museum, the site of the original concentration camp that had been housed in a series of old Polish army barracks. Time unfortunately was pressing, but the short while they spent in the museum was enough for someone like H.D., who had neither forgotten nor tried to forget the nightmarish terror. The horrendous things exhibited at the museum sufficed to give body to what he had heard and read—one room alone was filled with nothing but the eyeglasses of victims!

They spent only a few overwhelming minutes in Birkenau, the actual site of the gigantic death machine, with that enormous entrance and those deadly railroad tracks—photos of which have been printed thousands and thousands of times.

The visitors drove back to Krakow in silence.

At about 4 p.m. on the same day, H.D. and Luisa left for Wroclaw. They arrived half an hour early to be on the safe side. The station was being reconstructed, and things were so chaotic that they managed only at the very last moment to jump onto the train and settle down in a first-class compartment. When they reached Katowice, H.D. wanted to see if there was a dining car at the head of the train. Pushing his way up the platform through the bustling mass of people, he managed to reach the head of the train and jump on just as it started pulling out of the station again. This was a fleeting foretaste of the shock he was about to experience. He now had to fight his way through the incredible masses of people on the train to get back to his own compartment. People were sitting, standing, lying in the corridor and with each step H.D.

had to struggle not to step on someone. But everyone seemed in a good mood. After wrestling his way through the seven or eight cars for over twenty minutes—and by now at the end of his rope—he finally got back to the compartment he thought was his. But it wasn't. In his struggle to get through the crowd, or perhaps because in Katowice new passengers had entered the compartment, he must have missed seeing Luisa. He had no choice but to keep on looking, and finally, increasingly distressed, arrived at the end of the long corridor. He was about to open the door to the next car when—to his horror—he saw bright, flashing railroad tracks outside! Terror shot through his body, and in his mind's eye he saw once more the tracks of Birkenau that had filled him with fear only a few hours before.

It was obvious now that Luisa was sitting in a part of the train that had been uncoupled in Katowice. He pictured her all alone, surrounded by their luggage (to which she had substantially contributed) and most probably with very little money. Her part of the train was probably also heading for Wroclaw, but with God knows what delays and detours! How were they going to find each other again?

H.D. found a young man who could stammer a few phrases of English and begged him for help. He assured H.D. that none of the cars had been left back in Katowice, and that H.D. should make his way back toward the engine. Shaking with fear, he set off once more looking for Luisa, and found her, sitting with a smile on her face just two compartments down. "Where have you been all this time?" she asked. H.D. collapsed silently into his seat, his fear slowly evaporating as he told her what had happened. Traces of this fear lingered for days.

They arrived in Wroclaw that evening as planned and

were welcomed warmly at the charming, slightly frayed Hotel Monopol. They were now ready to set off for their original destination—Krakow and Auschwitz having been last-minute diversions—Kreisau.

Until 1945, the Kreisau estate had belonged to H.J. von Moltke, the central figure in one of Germany's most comprehensive Resistance movements. The Gestapo called the group the *Kreisau Kreis*, the Kreisau circle. H.D. had not belonged to this group, but he had been in constant contact with von Moltke, his brother-in-law, who was the same age. Between March 1942 and November 1944, H.D.'s civilian war work took him regularly to the gigantic construction sites of Upper Silesia's chemical plants. With all the horrendous things he was finding out, Kreisau had become a sort of moral sanctuary. After 1944, when von Moltke was arrested, H.D.'s main motive for going there was to visit his sister.

It was five months short of forty-seven years later that he was returning to Kreisau, to walk in the radiant sunshine in the company of four women he cherished—a sister, a wife, a daughter, and his sister's granddaughter. The day before, in a heavy downpour, he had been to the crumbling castle and had seen the stables whitewashed for the meeting between Chancellor Helmut Kohl and Prime Minister Tadeusz Mazowiecki. H.D. had gone there in a bus full of Germans and Poles, all eager to turn Kreisau into an international crossroads, but to H.D. this was of little importance. His own Kreisau he was going to see the following day.

The open country was the way it had always been, and the "Berghaus," where his sister had lived, was in good condition. H.D. glanced up lovingly at the rooms in which he had stayed. The small, platformless, train station was the same as it had always been. They were given a tour of the house by an old Polish man who, during the war, had been in the Polish Legion and had gone by way of Russia, Iraq, and Egypt to Italy for two years and remembered a little Italian. The sun was still shining radiantly, and H.D. and the women went down the familiar road to the station where they were photographed, his sister throwing her arms around him, just as she had done forty-seven years before. It was such a moving experience—and so vivid—that reliving it was a source of pure joy.

September 1991

THE GREEN TALBOT

"*Vous avez causé, n'est pas*!?" The Parisian bus driver grinned down at the green Talbot from the bus window, glassless in those days, with a mixture of compassion and surprise. The bus was parked in front of the *Orangerie*. Its huge front wheel had dented the Talbot's fender.

It was late afternoon on an August day in 1934. The newlywed chronicler, H.D., and his equally newlywed wife, Dickie, hadn't been goofing around at all—their worn tires had simply skidded on the rain-drenched asphalt, and their ancient car had slid against the bus. There were only three days left before they were to set off on their honeymoon, a trip for which H.D. had saved extra vacation days from work. They managed in the nick of time to fix the fender and quickly apply some green paint—the same color as the rest of the car.

How had this young couple, who had everything in life except money, managed to get their hands on a car that was "almost" their own? The background of their arrival in Paris and their marriage has already been set forth in an earlier episode, "Four Plates in Pieces." Since May 1, 1934, H.D. had been working for the French branch of I.G. Farben. Fate, as always, was kind to him: he had barely set foot on Parisian soil when a Nazi co-worker—a "local group leader"—was fired for embezzlement, and H.D. took over his position.

(It was well known that the Nazi regime had set up such "local groups" of the Party in all of the world's major cities for the surveillance of Germans abroad and for general espionage.) H.D.'s new job brought him a new friend, a Slovenian about ten years older than he, who had lived in Paris quite a while and who later, during the war, was to become an important informant for Helmuth James von Moltke.

In 1934, there were two things missing in Zdenko Sajovic's life: a wife and a driver's licence with accompanying car. H.D. could only help him secure the latter. However, as a result of H.D.'s attempts to teach him to drive, their budding friendship might have collapsed if they had not found a secondhand car and quickly registered it under Zdenko's name. It was a convertible, light-green four seater, whose make—Talbot—was the only thing about it that inspired any confidence. Its indeterminate age and unknown number of miles-travelled justified its low price. But, as we shall see, in the six months that followed, the Talbot did offer pretty good service.

H.D. was twenty-seven, and Dickie twenty-two—the perfect ages for enjoying their new life together. They were in Paris, far away from Nazi Germany, learning a new language, settling into a new job. They had their own apartment, were busy planning their married life, and were about to set off on their first trip together. One might think that under these circumstances they would not have had time for anything that did not directly concern them. Wrong! Their happiness was overshadowed by the horrendous day-to-day developments in Germany. What was so frightening was not only the injustice that was affecting their friends back home, but the horrible realization that their worst nightmares were coming true.

The Nazis, in the first months after they came to power, duped the world into believing that they were legitimate. The

Röhmputsch, which Hitler and his cohorts launched on June 30, 1934, however, left everyone stunned. Political opponents were picked out of the ranks with unscrupulous calculation and murdered in cold blood. Goebbels managed to play down—even justify—what had happened. Yes, it had been a blood bath, he announced, but a blood bath that had been necessary to stop a coup d'etat. To this day, H.D. is at a loss as to why the French press swallowed Goebbels' explanation with such docility that within a few days everyone had forgotten the incident. In Paris, it was impossible to find out exactly what had happened, or even the full list of those murdered. It was also impossible to determine how the Germans themselves were reacting to these "politically justified" murders.

Shortly after the *Röhmputsch*, H.D.'s "Grosser Onkel" came to Paris. (Not only was this uncle tall and the head of the family, but also quite big in the sense that he was one of the seven movers and shakers of I.G. Farben—all in all a rather charming, highly-educated man.) H.D. wanted to know exactly what had happened and how many people had been murdered.

"Well," the uncle answered, "if they want to kill each other, its fine with us!"

H.D. was left speechless by such cynicism, and was shocked to see a year later that his uncle's initial cynical distance from the Nazis had turned into downright collaboration.

In 1935 his uncle had returned to Paris to attend the Derby at Longchamps, which was held on the last Sunday in June. He went every year wearing his fashionable cutaway— even Hitler would not have been able to stop him. Strangely enough, he himself was averse to riding. Not so his wife, whom H.D. held in the highest esteem. A libretto of Nazi songs lying as an alibi on her coffee table, she rode exclusively "aryanized" horses, and was still riding these horses in

1942. (It would be an interesting sociocritical question to discover how these dubiously aryan horses might have escaped the concentration camps!) The long and short of it was that his aunt fell from a horse and injured herself so badly that she was on crutches when she came to visit occupied France along with all the other German wives and bosses. Rumor had it that she was there to smooth over the social problems that the work-force of the French companies controlled by I.G. Farben might have.

She was met at the Gare de l'Est by a friend of H.D.'s, whom he had hired for I.G. Farben three years earlier with the stipulation: "If you are anti-Nazi, you can have the job."

"I injured myself while working for the Red Cross," H.D.'s aunt announced.

"I am so sorry, madam. But I wasn't aware that one could carry out one's Red Cross duties on horseback," H.D.'s friend answered. The aunt smiled icily. He was never again called upon to carry out such sensitive missions. The reader will understand that the chronicler could not resist sharing this truly historic vignette even though now we will have to jump back seven years to 1935, where this piece began.

That year, H.D.'s uncle encouraged the young couple to come to the Derby at Longchamps—it would be a sin to miss such an opportunity, he argued, to hobnob with the *crème de la crème*. They weren't quite sure if they really wanted to hobnob, but they were curious, and agreed to go along. However, when it came to dressing up for the occasion they began worrying a little. On the one hand they didn't wish to clash with their uncle's cutaway. On the other hand they found the whole thing rather inappropriate given the times and didn't want to show-off before the thousands of regular spectators. But the day at the Derby did have its good side. The experience was like a bucket of ice water. H.D. reacted just as he had eight years earlier in Munich, where he spent a whole winter season dancing with the white-gloved daughters of the Bavarian aristocracy. Both experiences immunized him against temptations of that kind.

Before H.D. and Dickie set off on their motoring tour of Central Europe, there had been another important "immunization"—H.D.'s first and last shoplifting venture. He and his charming wife were living in a small furnished apartment in one of the side streets off Avenue de la Grande Armée, and they did all their shopping on Avenue de Ternnes. One of the first supermarkets had just sprung up there, and the young couple bought a double-necked cruet for vinegar and oil. The moment they got home one of the glass stoppers fell off the bottle and shattered on the tiles of the kitchen floor. What were they to do? The cruet had been too expensive for them to just forget it. So H.D. went back to the supermarket and swiped the glass stopper from one of the bottles still patiently waiting to be sold. He was so overcome with remorse at having left the poor bottle standing there decapitated that he never stole again.

In mid-August, the couple finally set off on their long-planned car trip. Their first goal was a lake in Austria's Salzkammergut called the Grundlsee, and one could get there quite easily without having to cut into Nazi Germany. The green Talbot now took center stage as they set off in the direction of Sens. Overcast and drizzling weather gave way to darkness and, the moment H.D. turned on the headlights, the car stalled. H.D.'s heart skipped a beat. The damn Talbot should have at least held out until they got to Austria, where they'd have no trouble finding a garage. As they fiddled with the car, they realized that if Dickie pressed her hand lightly on the dashboard, the engine would run just fine—proof, yet again, that two are better than one. There was no point in pushing their luck, however, so they decided to stop over in Sens and wait for the morning before proceeding. By noon the following day, the Talbot swung its way up the Grimsel-pass, rolled steeply down into the valley on the other side, and then climbed just as steeply up the Furkapass, where they intended to stop for lunch. They got there safe and sound, but only after suffering a bit of a shock. As the Talbot pointed its nose up the pass, it filled the whole valley floor with a cloud of deep-blue exhaust. It was obvious that the engine was burning oil and the size of the cloud convinced them that the car was about to breathe its last. "Its a lost cause!" H.D. said, "but we might as well drive on." As they climbed the mountain the exhaust cloud began to evaporate, and soon all three arrived in one piece at the top of the pass.

Back then, cars were few and far between in the mountains, and the Talbot innocently parked itself next to an enormous black Maybach limousine—at the time, the most expensive and technically advanced car in Europe. (They were manufactured in limited numbers in Constance by the Zeppelin factory. Its engine was so powerful that it needed only two gears, instead of the usual four.) H.D. asked the driver how he had come up the pass ("I just put it in first!"), and also asked to whom the car belonged ("Privy Counselor Bosch"). The answer delighted H.D.: here was the mightiest man of I.G. Farben, with the mightiest car, next to the smallest employee with the most dilapidated. Privy Counselor Bosch did not have to check his oil, but H.D. did, and realized that the green Talbot had lost all its oil over just five hundred kilometers. The car did, however, easily roll down the mountain to the next gas station, and thereafter the loose pistons did their best as H.D. tackled two more Alpine passes, the Arlberg near Innsbruck and the Pötschen near Bad Aussee. When they finally arrived at the Grundlsee, the Talbot dug in its heels, and for the next two weeks stepped out of the lime-light—except for a few appointments at the mechanic's.

Their arrival at the Grundlsee will remain etched forever in H.D.'s memory. There they were, H.D. and Dickie, a solid couple, back together in the cozy warmth of the world of their friends Genia and Hermann Schwarzwald. H.D. and Dickie had both, in their own way and at different times (Dickie a few years later than H.D.), been fashioned by that environment, and both were convinced that the world at large should ideally be like that of their friends. They were convinced that what you had to do was go out and try to make it so.

H.D. had spent summer vacations at the Grundlsee since 1927. He knew every person, animal, and plant in the area, and all the regular guests at the Seeblick, an old hotel that Genia Schwarzwald had turned into a summer camp where older people could unbutton and younger people could expe-rience what cultivated freedom was all about.

The first few days were spent meeting old friends and enjoying the harmonious blend of landscape and people. But things at the Grundlsee had changed. Everyone was aware of the dark events of the past two months: the murders in Ger-many and the dissolution of the Austrian Parliament by the Austro-fascists, followed two weeks later by the assassina-tion of Austrian Chancellor Dollfuss by Nazi commandos. (For the fact that they chased away the Nazis—albeit tempo-rarily—one must begrudgingly thank the Austro-fascists.)

By now, the people staying at the Seeblick were no longer just emigrés. Many of them were political exiles. Fraudoktor—that is how everyone addressed Genia Schwarzwald—would get stacks of mail from all over the world, including cries of help from destitute friends. She did manage to help a few of them, but, alas, only a few. H.D. had learned a hard lesson. In his seven years as a member of the Schwarzwald set, he had never asked who was Jewish and who was not. The only Jews he knew were Jews who were fully assimilated; he saw no difference between them and everybody else. But all of a sudden, he was expected to see a difference, even if it was only that the Jews were singled-out and he wasn't.

The vacation at the Grundlsee was beautiful despite all of this, but was quickly over. H.D. and Dickie now had to brace themselves for the journey back into a harsher world. The green Talbot once more took center stage. The Austrian mechanics had cured its inner afflictions, but had not done much for its appearance. Their first stop was in Frankfurt, where they had to hide the car in a side street from the critical eyes of the newly privileged Nazis.

They were in Frankfurt because a relative had asked them to be in her wedding procession, a request that H.D. could not refuse for all sorts of family reasons. The procession marched from the bride's parental home in a residential area to the church, about five hundred meters away. H.D. and his wife, as one of the younger couples and not part of the immediate family, were waiting to follow in the back of the procession. This gave them ample opportunity to observe the marchers and whisper discreet comments to each other. In a sense, it was a historic march. Who would have believed a year and a half prior to the beneficent and order-restoring seizure of power that such a "capitalistic" wedding procession could move freely and undisturbed through the streets of a large city. But move it did—it was obvious that there were quite a few people around who were enjoying the "new liberties" of this kind that Nazism had brought with it.

As was the custom, the beaming bride and her father led the procession. Initially, her choice of husband hadn't gone down too well with her parents. The bridegroom-to-be was unemployed, and as for his reputed Ph.D. from the University of Leipzig, a great-aunt (a staunch anti-Nazi) living in Leipzig had not managed, however hard she tried, to locate his dissertation. Counterbalancing these uncertainties, however, was the fact that he was a member of the staff of Ernst Röhm, chief of staff of the SA and one of the main players in the Nazi takeover. In his continuing association with Röhm fate smiled on him. When Röhm and his men were executed on June 30 on the banks of one of Bavaria's lakes, the groom happened to have taken a few days off. On learning of this he was quick to throw himself into the arms of the murderers—the SS—and thanks to his father-in-law's relationship with the Nazi foreign minister, von Neurath, landed a position in the foreign service. In the procession, the groom (it has slipped H.D.'s mind which of his uniforms he was wearing) walked arm in arm with his somewhat embarrassed-looking mother.

Then came the show-stopper of the procession—the bride's mother! She wore a long dark-green velvet dress, a tiara, and was amply yet tastefully bedecked with jewelry. It was as if she had stepped out of a Gainsborough painting: the lady of the manor back from a ride over the moors. It was she who garnered the spectators' applause—which she ostensibly felt rightfully hers. After the wedding, the procession gathered again outside the church, but this time with the newlyweds in front, their parents, bubbling over with emotion, following close behind.

All H.D. remembers from this point on is the married

couple driving off—after a sumptuous meal—in an enormous, shiny, dark-blue Horch-Kabriolet (secondhand, people whispered). H.D. and Dickie escaped to their hidden green Talbot, managing that same night, with a deep sigh of relief, to cross the French border.

October 1991

The Silver Cup

The silver cup came into the life of the chronicler, H.D., over eighty-four years ago and is today in as good condition as it was on that very first day. It has the following measurements: the diameter of its base is 47 millimeters, its drinking rim 65 millimeters, with a conical, unornamented stem of 87 millimeters. Its weight is 180 grams. Anyone studying it would notice immediately that it is a cup in the style of art-nouveau, and see that the faded, barely legible monogram reads "H.D." Its inside once had a touch of gold, which, with its owner, it has gradually lost over the years. Had it been of less elegant shape, it would surely have led the life of a run-of-the-mill cup. But owing to its beauty, H.D. had many replicas of it made so that others too could enjoy its services. Thus the silver cup became quite naturally a symbol of a community spirit in everyday undertakings.

True, it is first and foremost a baptismal cup, a quality it has hung on to with iron, if not silver, conviction. It was brought into the family by H.D.'s godmother, a friend of his mother's.

For the first two years, until H.D. could hold it in his own little hands, it most probably had to wait patiently in the cupboard. Then things got going. For a long time H.D. drank from it at table, but suddenly, one day—the family was still living in the old ancestral home—the cup took on another function: assisting in the daily brushing of H.D.'s teeth. After 1951, the cup often took breaks from this function, but only when it had to be measured to make replicas whose mission it was to welcome newborn children of friends and colleagues. That the cup would take on symbolic weight became clear only as the years rolled on.

Carlo Vezzelli is the artist who, over the years, has replicated the cup. He is an energetic and witty Milanese, a gold- and silversmith working in a top-floor atelier at No. 2 Via Montenapoleone, who pursues his art with sharp and discerning enthusiasm. (Only the other day he said to H.D.: "You haven't changed a bit, still not a single blond hair on your head!")

Discerning readers will by now be saying to themselves, "You can brush your teeth whatever way you like, but please don't burden us with the details." H.D.'s reply, however, is that the cup, just like he himself and so many others, came into its own only after a life full of protracted detours. The cup turned into a symbol of life in Italy at forty-four years of age. This is the first time that this idea has been put into words— the cup, as is its nature, only silently smiles its approval.

After weeks of doubt and uncertainty, H.D. is still not sure if he is capable of explaining to the reader, and to himself, what led him and his wife to leave Germany in 1948 and move to Italy forever.

It had been more than just the need for a steady income, a need which had become urgent by the summer of 1948. By then the money he had been paid in June as president of Bad Homburg's de-Nazification court was about to run out. He could have done well in Germany by returning to his prewar profession (I.G. Farben), but the last thing he wanted was to be thrust back into that corner.

In Milan, at the end of 1950, H.D. ran into his former I.G. Farben supervisor, an intelligent, run-of-the-mill Nazi supporter, not much older than H.D., who had now landed himself a job with Bayer. He had the audacity to say that the war had only briefly interrupted work and that everything was back to normal. H.D., happy in his newly gained freedom, refrained from commenting, but tactfully made it clear to his former boss that they weren't going to be exchanging Christmas cards. He gladly did without the Bayer dyestuffs account. (This manager was the same man who, on the day France fell in 1940, had said to H.D.: "This is the first time you actually look happy, so I see that you too are all for the war." H.D.'s answer: "Yes! Because now it may be over!" The manager had answered him with an uncomprehending shake of the head.)

As important as it is to earn one's keep, man cannot live by bread alone, as Eugen Rosenstock Huessy so charmingly remarked. After the war, H.D. had returned "victorious" to Germany, filled with hopes for all the new (not "restored"!) possibilities that he might find there. Three years later, he was severely disappointed: there was no spiritual cohesion among the German people, and they were not prepared to accept responsibility for Nazism—a key element for any serious renewal of Germany. Solidarity was totally lacking. One could argue that things got somewhat better later, but H.D. had been waiting since he was twenty-six. Fifteen years, he thought to himself, was long enough.

Confusion in knowledge and conscience knew no bounds. Self-defense against the notion of "collective guilt" took on the comfortable sophistry that if one is "collectively" guilty then he is thereby immune from any individual responsibility. It was predictable that just as after the First World

War people fell back on the legend of the "stab in the back"—
the rulers, after all, are always innocent—people fell back on
"collective guilt" after the Second World War; the one legend
aggressive, the other defensive.

The idea of establishing small, genuine communities that
could start building up a new Germany was turned down by
the allies (it was mistakenly identified with the Nazi *Volk*-
community concept). The Allies then added to the confusion
by resuscitating the hapless Weimar parties and launching on
an idiotic "de-Nazification" sweep. This plan was stupid
because it targeted scores of "innocent" minor members of
the Nazi party and turned out to be nothing more than a
time-consuming ordeal that gave real criminals and their
henchmen ample time to escape.

In cases where dodging collective guilt was not possible, point-blank forgiveness was demanded, without considering the fact that across-the-board forgiveness was just
as collective and therefore unfeasible. (For example, *I can't
forgive* the Nazis for the murder of my neighbor's mother.)

Many years later, after having been time and again asked
why he left Germany, H.D. coined for himself the honorary
title "Adenauer Refugee."

(Digression: Forty-two years after the war we have a
replay of "West" Germany's arrogance and intolerance, qualities by which the Germans themselves are convinced to be
unblemished: In 1991, a friend and contemporary of H.D.'s
pointed out that in 1945 the Germans had only twelve years
of Nazism to put behind them and consequently were quite
aware of what had to be done, while East Germans had to
contend with fifty-nine years of darkness and now had to
face the somewhat dubious light of German reunification
without having a valid past of their own to hold onto.)

Germany's painful shortcomings after 1945 were not the proximate cause for H.D.'s leaving his country forever. The push came from Italy where friends and acquaintances from the Italian resistance and from his prewar work there, were interested in importing once more the type of chemicals that I.G. Farben had distributed chiefly to the leather and textile industries. They were convinced that H.D. was the right man to start negotiations with the companies that took over I.G. Farben (it turned out that they were right). At first H.D. was unconvinced. He was however flattered, because the invitation had come from Italy, the land to which, after three years of battling evil, he felt more closely bound than to his fatherland, against which for twelve years he had constantly to defend himself. He was also, after all, unemployed . . .

In the second half of 1948, H.D. put politics on the back burner. The single most important task was to focus all his energy on building a new life, both from a material and a spiritual standpoint. At the beginning, he was still somewhat uncertain, but his instinct, enriched through his experiences in Italy, led him to believe that in his work he was going to be able to connect the material and the ethical better than he had been able to do before. Much of what had taken place inside him in the past few years still had to be worked through. He had not wanted to accept that the alienation, a consequence of what had taken place in the war and the ensuing problematic decisions he had to take, would continue. He felt that Italy would heal that.

H.D.'s Italian friends invited him to come to Milan, to convince him that he was indispensable to the plans they intended to carry out. At home then in Germany, H.D. told his wife:

"There's nothing in Italy—at least, there's very, very

little. Let's go there!" Everyone asked him if he felt he could get along better with the Italians than with the Germans. He loved this question, because he could answer it so heartily in the affirmative. Once the Italians overcome their well-justified anti-German feelings (by the way, it is funny how both Germans and Jews tend to evoke the same strange blend of admiration and aversion) they are free of prejudice and definitely free of arrogance. They are neither capricious nor indifferent, but they are very responsive. Certain individuals might be lacking in discipline, but they are masters of improvisation and are not tied down by rules. Italians are quick and sharp, qualities they don't let go to their heads; When motivated they are excellent workers. Italians have a good relationship with their past because they do not try to gloss over the mistakes and crimes that were committed. One must never act superior with them—after all, one isn't.

To recreate what was happening in Germany back then, the chronicler had to supplement his memories with research. He found a substantial amount of material, little of which, however, had any direct bearing on his own life. In the spring of 1947, the three Western Allies had met in Moscow and agreed that Germany would not have to pay a war indemnity, and in July the Marshall Plan was put into effect. On June 1, it had been decided that the three German Western zones would come under that plan's jurisdiction. On June 18, 1948, the *Deutschmark* was born, and with it the doors to German trade opened. That was a decisive factor in H.D.'s work in Milan. But Italy was not yet ready to lift its embargo on Germany, nor was it clear whether H.D.'s residence permit would be extended. Both these factors sent him to Rome in January 1949. On the evening of his first, rather unsuccessful, day there H.D. sought solace by going into the nearest movie theater. Within minutes, he realized that the movie was about a North African man who had not been granted residency in France. H.D.—in a flash of *"mors tua vita mea"* philosophy—saw it as a good omen.

At noon on November 5, 1948, fate had nearly managed to throw a wrench into H.D.'s wheel of fortune. In Bellinzona, he and his family narrowly escaped a head-on collision with a Swiss car. In his pocket diary he had noted: "5 p.m. arrival in Maccagno" (on Lake Maggiore). For the next ten months, the immigrants settled into a friend's small summer villa H.D. had known from the last year of the war.

In November 1948, H.D. walked up a small flight of stairs at Via Podgora 13 (100 meters away from Milan's Palace of Justice), which led from a shadowy courtyard to the mezzanine. He had just become employee #9 and was to inspect the four small offices of the newly established import firm, SASEA. Little did he or anyone else know that those were the first steps toward the creation of a community spirit that was to be his daily commitment for the next twenty-five years.

The acronym SASEA was meaningless, because the company never actually had anything to do with solventi, "solvents," or *ed Affini*, "and related products." It dealt, rather, with dyes, pigments, and other synthetic materials. The chronicler does not intend to give the full commercial history of SASEA—his aim is to discuss how and why, with much input from everyone, a special "community" evolved. At the end of every month, the sales results were reported and were usually excellent. A close colleague recently reminded H.D. how they all used to celebrate these events with H.D. bringing *Boeri*, liqueur-filled chocolates, from the café across the street.

As a result of all the successes, the pleats of the SASEA skirt had to be constantly let out. In 1950, the company expanded into Via Matteo Bandello, where in the course of the next few years additional offices were secured in the same building and in the building across the street. The colleagues gave up their "freedom" only in 1976 when BASF—significantly, a German concern—took over.

What freedom? Inner and outer, based on unrestricted respect of and to one another. Of course there had always been *dirigenti*—managers—in the company, but the credo was not to give workers orders but convince them of the validity of what was at hand. Free and open expression of opinion was a general prerequisite. Readiness to help each other was another important "freedom," which was part not only of the job but also of the sharing of one another's highs and lows. What was particularly valuable was the freedom felt via-à-vis the Germans—not only, as one might think, for the owners of SASEA, but for everyone working there. At work, the only weapon the Germans had left was persuasion. In order to keep SASEA independent, the shareholders deposited their shares with a trustee in Zurich, with the stipulation that in the case of a breach of contract the majority of SASEA stocks would go to BASF.

"But you're putting yourselves completely in our hands!" a BASF lawyer uttered in disbelief. He was obviously not well versed in what "freedom" is all about.

"Not in the least!" H.D. retorted. "We at SASEA aim to satisfy BASF, but still keep our freedom!" Silent amazement was the response.

One Saturday afternoon—in those days we still had six-day weeks—H.D. was met outside the office by his wife. She exclaimed: "All the people coming out of the SASEA offices are smiling, while everyone else's faces are downcast!" She was no doubt exaggerating, but it was nice to hear anyway.

The smiles were in part due to the fact that at SASEA we tried to grant higher wages and longer vacations than the official standards, taking into account both work quality and individual needs.

Sales continued to improve, and by the late summer of 1949 H.D. could buy himself a new fountain pen. Two main factors boosted the business: SASEA traded in commodities that were very scarce and had good technicians—two of the founders and an assistant—who due to their traditional German schooling before the war knew exactly what they were offering.

Throughout this time, the SASEA colleagues grew closer to each other, and so it was no surprise that the *silver cup* came onto the scene. Its first mission, on November 15, 1951, was to remind Patrizia P. for the rest of her life that all the SASEA colleagues had celebrated her birth that day. There are differing estimates of how many silver cups became the symbol of the SASEA community in the following two decades—some say twenty-five, some say thirty.

The cup itself can't be forgotten, its metallic form sees to that. But the quality and scope of the colleagues' relationship with one another can only live on in memory, with one priceless exception. One of the colleagues took it upon herself to gather a comprehensive collection of documents relating to the many company events between the years 1956 and 1970: Christmas dinners, the distribution of presents to children, and annual company trips.

Here are some of the company get-togethers:

The careful seating arrangements at Christmas dinners were of vital importance. H.D. and his assistants were veritable masters of ceremony and invariably had the satisfaction of knowing that they had managed to seat all present without anyone feeling slighted. At the center was the president, Enrico

Hintermann, highly esteemed by all, and surrounded by the guests of honor. All the other big and small *dirigenti* (executives) were distributed throughout the dining room, so that even those who had a somewhat higher opinion of themselves could still interact harmoniously with the rest. "Have I told you today how much I like you?" a highly respected teacher living in Vienna before 1938 used to say to her pupils. At SASEA—H.D. felt this right from the start—everyone was both teacher and student, managing time and again to express their high esteem for each other.

But wait—it's not that SASEA was something special, or that its workers were angels. Nor for H.D. was it a career institute. Fate had simply put him in a position to keep this initially small but rapidly booming enterprise together. Without wanting to, he became its helmsman, a man of unintentional intent. He was lucky in that most of those sharing his work also saw their main aim as being the furthering of the group "materially and ethically." Experience had led everyone to the conviction that interacting well led to the best results for all involved. An example: January 2, 1956, H.D. found a congratulatory message on his desk, which read: "For H.D.'s Silver Jubilee from I.G. Farben January 2, 1931. We the happy few whom fate has brought into your orbit wish to congratulate you from the depths of our heart. We are thankful to I.G. Farben for the opportunity of having inherited you." Which of the by now one hundred and fifty-seven coworkers, all of whom had signed the card, had initiated this action will remain forever a state secret. Moved, H.D. could only thank them with the words: "Let us all go on liking each other!"

But the chronicler does not wish to be hypocritical. The harmony at SASEA required hard work on all sides. After all, whenever one has so many people working in such close quarters, there will be incidents of quarreling, egoism, and envy. But the main thing was that there were also, at all levels of the company, responsible peacemakers. In 1969, H.D. had written in his pocket diary, "Had words today with X. For more than twenty years I have refused to see him as a despicable fellow, but he really is despicable!" You see—for twenty years, for the good of the group, H.D. had managed to like even such a character as X.

In 1957 and again in 1962, SASEA went on three-day company trips to Germany to visit their clients (Cassella in Frankfurt and BASF in Ludwigshafen). Both trips were designed to counter the corporate anonymity between northern and southern collaborating firms and to help lift the slight diffidence the Italians felt toward the Germans as well as strengthen the Germans' trust of their Italian partners. The trips were a success and confirmed the organizer's concept—working together afterward took on a new dimension.

All the other company trips between 1956 and 1970, among them trips to Paris, Vienna, Sicily, Elba, Sardinia, Yugoslavia, and Switzerland, were "motive-less," true vacations.

In 1965, the group stayed on the Italian mainland. The weather was bad throughout the trip, so they decided to lighten the mood by having a "Mr. and Miss SASEA" contest while the rain outside drummed on the windowpanes. H.D. begs the reader's forgiveness for no longer remembering who was voted "Miss SASEA"—there were so many pretty girls in the firm. But the "Mr. SASEA" vote got stalled. It was clear that young Antonio, Battista's chief assistant, was the most attractive and best liked among the men. The unanimous vote was about to fall on him when he rushed up flustered to H.D., asking him to intervene to make C., Battista's second assistant, a perfectly nice but somewhat plain lad hired just a month before, "Mr. SASEA" instead of him—"He so desperately needs the prize, a pair of shoes."

The following little incident illustrates well how un-dictatorial things were at SASEA. One of H.D.'s uncles came down to Milan from Germany and was brought to his office by Battista. As always in the late afternoon, H.D. was still immersed in work and asked him to wait. Various coworkers breezed in and out the office with a quick "Permesso?" Some needed a signature, others a decision, and others again just wanted to report new developments. Suddenly during a small pause in the flow, H.D.'s uncle asked him: "Who's actually running this firm?" "Why?—I am!" It seems that the uncle had never before come across such an un-directorial director. He didn't say a word, but looked skeptically at H.D., doubtful that things would work out. But things were working out. For the first twenty years after the war, Italy, through SASEA, was the most important European export country for BASF, and SASEA managed to work at a lower cost than BASF's own branch in France. All this, to a large extent, thanks to the silver cup.

From early on, H.D. had been on the lookout for a successor who would advance both SASEA and the cup's good work. H.D.'s choice was satisfactory from a business standpoint; but the cup and its congenial charisma soon dropped out of the picture. At the beginning of the 1970s, a new law prescribed the institution of employees' councils, modeled on the workers' councils. H.D. immediately supported the idea of setting up such a council so that the company could continue doing what up until now had been achieved under the influence of the silver cup, in a legally prescribed way: nurture trust! The "new" Germans, however, turned the suggestion

down. It would be best, they argued, to wait till the employees (no longer colleagues!) demanded the formation of such
a council. The result was the birth of mistrust at SASEA.

H.D. stuck to his original time schedule and retired in
1975; not to sit back and relax, but to dedicate himself fully
to the third phase of his life. Of the second phase of his life—
his work at SASEA—he retained the happy memory of colleagues and friends who for so many years had selflessly ral-
lied around the silver cup.

In 1985, nine years after BASF had slipped into SASEA's
well-tailored suit, H.D. was asked if he would like to take
part in a second reunion party (the first had taken place a
year earlier). It was to be a meeting of old colleagues, some
of them now working at other firms, others retired. Everyone
wanted to be up on the post-SASEA fate of their old friends
and to reminisce about the well-tailored suit they had all
helped fashion. (Of the 101 former colleagues, more than half
participated in this 1990 reunion.)

March 1990

THE WORKERS' FRONT CAP

The chronicler's main aim in the years between 1936 (when he returned from France) and 1942 (when he had to face the draft) was to keep as far away from Nazism as he possibly could. In other words, to challenge it in every way possible, even in seemingly trivial ways such as dodging the "Heil Hitler!" greeting. Today this seems hardly worth mentioning, but in those days it required a constant sense of responsibility. In any case, Nazism had to be kept away from body and soul at all costs. H.D. can attest with humble satisfaction that he did manage to avoid such guilt—except of course for the fact that he is still alive. There was, however, one compromise: he could not avoid the Workers' Front cap. (During the war he also enlisted in the *Volkswohlfahrt*, a Nazi welfare organization, in order to safeguard his wife from harassment by the Nazis.)

Nowadays people who hadn't been born before 1945 or, like German Chancellor Kohl, were "far too young at the time," cannot imagine what it took to protect one's integrity and the integrity of one's ever-diminishing circle of friends in the face of an evil, all-engulfing terror.

Some historians will only believe instances of Nazi terror where there are documents to back them up. For them, simple eyewitness-accounts will not suffice. Who would believe today that in January 1936, in I.G. Farben's Italian section, he was given a desk next to a scrawny little military-looking SA man, who often showed up in a cloud of alco-holic fumes wearing an SA-shirt. "When we took over," the SA man once told H.D., "We never tortured anyone! It was only when Communists wouldn't talk that we'd throw them in a cellar and fill it with water till they spilled the beans!"

H.D. managed to get this Nazi drunk relocated, after which only a few harmless sympathizers remained in the Italian section.

The workers' canteen was on a small hill about a hundred meters behind the enormous I.G. Farben office building in Frankfurt. About two thousand workers ate their lunch in two shifts on the ground level, while management and guests dined upstairs. Consequently, on the way to lunch one often ran into top directors and could exchange friendly greetings.

On a sunny autumn day in 1937, the general manager of the firm walked into the canteen, lifted his hand straight in front of him, and shouted "Heil Hitler!" Next to him, a military figure in a highly decorated red-and-gold army uniform lifted his hand to his peaked cap. H.D. immediately recognized the man as Marshal Werner von Blomberg, at the time still the Minister of War. (He was fired shortly after, in February 1938—it turned out that von Blomberg, with Hitler as his best man, had married a former "professional" woman, and Hitler was sensitive to the public's class-consciousness. Oddly enough, what subsequently clinched Blomberg's entry in the Bertelsmann dictionary was his contravention of social norms, and not his ineptness—he had, after all, been one of the first to herald Hitler. Even the general manager of I.G. Farben did not think much of him.)

Back then, H.D. saw the two men's calling out the Hitler

greeting as a symbol of I.G. Farben's ardent involvement in the preparation for the war that was to break out a year and a half later. In desperate need of comic relief, he thought of the crude verse scrawled on the wall of the men's room on the 5th floor.

> The German greeting loud and proud
> While peeing should not be allowed!
> To shout "Heil Hitler!" filled with exaltation,
> In this vile place: monstrous violation!

The men's room offered a perfect opportunity of undermining Nazi protocol. H.D. would enter, absentmindedly shout "Heil Hitler!" and then loudly rebuke himself. A sign had been put up in his department proclaiming: "Our greeting must always be the German greeting!" H.D. immediately had it removed. It was an outrage, he explained, to be told to do something that was so natural.

Otherwise things went well. One day, the wife of the general manager, his aunt, asked him to wait for her down by the main entrance. She came, she saw, she pecked him on the cheek, and from that day on H.D. was allowed to park right in the middle of the office block, a distinction not even accorded top managers and directors.

On the first floor of the sixth office wing was the room where the unusually large board of directors convened. In it stood a long table, about a meter and a half wide, that occupied the whole length of the room. Along its middle ran a line of bells every two meters or so. These bells were there, H.D. told guests, so that the aged board members could alert the others if they were having a stroke. The tour-guide told only very trusted guests that one could only reach the bell with a Hitler salute.

These are some of the very few memories of that period over which one can laugh. Laughing, even maliciously, was of the utmost importance as a way of surviving the unending stream of horror. One of these horrors was the relentless pressure on H.D. to become a member of the Nazi party or at least one of the many other brown-shirt organizations.

It must have been about 1937 when all managers of I.G. Farben who had not yet joined the party finally joined. In the wake of this general Nazification, H.D.'s uncle, wishing to clinch the position of general manager of I.G. Farben, left the NSKK (National Socialist Drivers' Corps) to become a member of both the SA and the Nazi party. "Now I'll have to get myself a new uniform!" he told H.D. "If you want to join the Drivers' Corps—and I strongly advise you to—I can let you have the pants of my old uniform. I've only worn them once or twice." The family laughed uneasily, and H.D. left it at that.

In those days his uncle, a Rhinelander like H.D., still maintained a distant and somewhat cynical smile on his lips when it came to Nazism. He had banked on being able to keep both his high social position and his managerial position at I.G. Farben unscathed by introducing a selected group of "deserving" Nazis into the upper ranks. He was in no way what you would imagine a Nazi to be. He wasn't a sympathizer either—he was far too intelligent and talented for that. He had a sharp, clear intellect, and was both a linguist and a witty conversationalist. It was a pleasure listening to him speak at management conferences; but unfortunately he was, like so many others of his class, a "collaborator" who ultimately did not manage to avoid becoming an accomplice.

H.D. had been in charge of the Italian sales department since 1938, but after four years in that position had yet to be promoted to chief clerk. In 1942, he once more took his request for promotion to the general manager—his uncle— who pointed out that although his request was soundly based, H.D. was, after all, not a party member. "In that case," H.D. told him point-blank, "I shall have to write a letter to the board of directors."

"No, you don't have to do that. I'll see that everything's put right."

The result was that in this case personal interest won out over the Nazi party interest. Shortly afterward, when H.D. was drafted, his wife was sent a larger allowance until the end of the war.

Let us return to 1938. In the early evening of November 9, the synagogues were set ablaze. In Frankfurt, there were as yet no high buildings, and H.D. had a bird's-eye view over the roofs of the city from his office on the fifth floor of the I.G. Farben building. It was already getting dark—the workday was about to end—and H.D. called Herr Gerner, a close colleague of his, to witness the horrendous crimes that were taking place. In 1945, Gerner reminded him that H.D., shaken, had said: "Herr Gerner—this is the end of Germany!"

Friday-evening concerts had been a Frankfurt institution for decades, and there was a concert on Friday, November 11, 1938—in other words, two days after *Kristallnacht*. On the whole, the audience was politically neutral—basically more in favor of human rights than pro-Nazi, and everyone went to the concert as usual, as did H.D. and his wife. He remembers how ashamed they and their friends were, and also how surprised (horrified, actually) to see Arthur von Weinberg, one of Frankfurt's best-known and most influential Jews, sitting in his box facing the orchestra as if nothing had happened. That summer, his brother, Carlo von Weinberg, had told H.D. about his trip to India, where he "advised the local Nazi leader of the party branch there what actions to take in order to keep Germany's best interests at heart." The von Weinberg brothers were not the only Jews who simply refused to believe what was actually happening.

Then "Judenfrei," Germans began the dark year 1939. All H.D. remembers is that he was completely immersed in steering clear of Nazism, when on May 1st I.G. Farben had its company march into the center of town. All employees were compelled to "voluntarily" wear a Workers' Front cap. H.D. will never forget the distressing sight of those men (no women were in evidence), mostly decent people, gathering there in their light overcoats under those stupid caps. March orders sounded and the idiotic procession began. It was the one and only time H.D. wore that cap.

The long-awaited war broke out. Horrifying even many of the Nazis. An increasingly heavy blackout descended on the streets, the houses, and people's minds. H.D.'s uncle, the one at I.G. Farben, announced in 1940 that thanks to his "glorious" Wiesbaden pillage of the French chemical industry, he had clinched Germany's leadership in the international dye market for this generation and the next. H.D.'s retort, that in that case they might as well close shop, merely brought a smile to the uncle's face. After Germany's victory, he assured H.D., there would be more than enough work to do.

As the chronicler has already reported in "Augusta and Topolino," his uncle's mind had become even more blinkered by April 1, 1944. The whole Eastern Front had begun swinging westward, a fact that did not hinder his uncle from taking H.D. aside to confide that he had glorious plans for H.D.'s career at I.G. Farben after the war. H.D. had not said a word.

At the end of August 1944, a month after the failed

attempt on Hitler's life on July 20th (a misfortunate event for all level-headed Germans), the general manager proclaimed his "great relief that no industrialists had been involved in the attempted assassination." Seven months later however, he confided how surprised he was that the American commander who took over the I.G. Farben building refused to shake his—the general manager's—hand! As it turned out, of those among I.G. Farben's management who were released early from Landsberg prison he was the only one who refused to fall back into a "work as usual" mode after the war, confessing to his sister, H.D.'s mother, that he had "made a mess" of everything.

But let's return to the blacked-out but not yet bombed-out first two years of the war. H.D.'s hatred for the Nazi government was so vehement that he did not want I.G. Farben, even though he didn't have much respect for it, to sign over a million reichsmarks as a "payment" for an investment in Italy. The Italian dye manufacturer ACNA (51% Montecatini and 49% I.G. Farben) had decided to increase its capital, and I.G. Farben was to participate. Now, fifty-five years later, H.D. has not been able to retrieve the files of this transaction in Milan, but he remembers that I.G. Farben managed to steer clear of the payment, thanks to his fierce battle with the ministry. (Anyone else at I.G. Farben would have let the immensely affluent company pay up without a second thought.) H.D. later calculated that he saved I.G. Farben five times the total salary he received in his fourteen years there!

After work every evening, H.D. took the suburban tram from Frankfurt back to Bad Homburg. It was always full, its inside lights almost completely blacked out except for a small crack through which a bulb faintly flickered. H.D. stood under the dim light for an hour each day, managing to read quite a number of books—all of Selma Lagerlöf and Gottfried Keller.

One sunny Saturday morning in autumn, he left his office and on his way to the tram-stop crossed the nearly empty street and walked over the bicycle lane. Suddenly a cyclist almost ran into him, stopped and got off his bike: "Lucky you jumped out of the way just in time!"

Ever since, H.D. has always tried hard to jump out of the way "just in time."

March 1993

Horse Rollers

The chronicler, H.D., put much thought into where in the text he should place the picture of the two "rollers" that make up the object of this piece. Should he put the picture before or after he fully described the rollers and what they stood for, both in the past and today? H.D. likes to keep his readers in suspense, in the hope of heightening their enjoyment of the finale of a piece, regardless whether it is a good

ending or a bad one, so he asks the reader to study the picture below.

What you see is a photocopier, which indicates that an office is involved. You will also notice that there are two long round wooden rods mounted on either side of the window. From the picture you can't tell that these rods rotate, but as you will see this is of vital importance to the story. What use could these rollers possibly have for the attorney whose office is pictured above? The answer: none at all! Why do they play such an important role for both the attorney and for H.D., who had long forgotten all about them? Because quite by chance they are a poignant symbol of the building and the spirit of the people, past and present, who have inhabited the house.

In May 1992, for the first time in sixty-three years, H.D. had the opportunity to travel to the Mechernich Woods in the Voreifel, fifty kilometers south of Cologne. From 1907 his parents had a country house there called Hombusch, with stables for horses. Because of financial problems, they reluctantly had to sell the estate in 1929.

To help the reader visualize the object at the center of this story, H.D. would first like to describe its setting. The house stood on a rise among wooded hills. It was a rectangular building made up of three interlocked structures with a wall enclosing an expansive courtyard, on the left side of which were the living quarters. The "grand" stables stood in front of the gate; a coachman and later, a forester lived above them. To the right was the hayloft, and below it were guest stables, a coach house, a storage room, a garage, the chauffeur's rooms, and kennels.

Now we've almost come to the horse rollers. After the First World War, the west side of the house was enlarged, and the kitchen and pantries were moved. As there were no more horses around, the "grand" stables were refurbished as the kitchen area. Originally, there had been an entrance to these stables from the courtyard, and this entrance had been too narrow, so that wooden rollers had to be installed to insure that the horses wouldn't injure themselves as they crowded into the stables. When the stables were turned into a kitchen, the horse gate became the window seen in the picture. It hadn't occurred to the builders to remove the now useless rollers. In the seventy years that followed, the various people living in the house left the rollers were they were. They became a symbol of the continuity of the spirit of the house.

The present owners have been kind enough to take H.D. on a tour of the house, and it was then that he came upon the rollers against which the last horse's flanks had brushed seventy-eight years earlier. He could not resist running his fingers softly over the curve of the wood, and the rollers became magic wands bringing many memories back to life.

The riding horses went to war in 1914 when H.D. was only seven years old, and yet he still remembers how a year earlier his father, because of a leg injury, had had to be lifted onto a horse, and how his mother and the two small boys had clapped.

During the war, only one horse, Lisa, remained (in the guest stables). Lisa could not make up her mind, try as she might, whether she was a normal carriage horse or a field horse, which is what one used to call workhorses in the days before tractors. One of Lisa's duties was to transport the people of the house, including trips to and from the station at Mechernich. Driving down into the valley usually went smoothly, Lisa keeping up a quick trot. But riding up to Mechernich was painfully slow. The trip took about three-quarters of an hour in an open hunting carriage—two could sit in front on the box seat, and three more "hunters" could fit in the back.

In the first few years after World War I, the main playground for the children was the "rock," about a quarter of a mile away from the house, on the wooded path that led up to the Feyer's mill. Carl, H.D.'s brother, ruled the valley, allowing little Freya to reside in one of the villas on his domain. Carl kept a sharp eye out for H.D., who sought independence high up on the rock.

On September 9, 1917, the children's fun on the rock was abruptly interrupted by an invitation from the Feyer's mill. They were throwing a party to celebrate H.D.'s tenth birthday. There, at the very end of the Hombusch estate, stood a small, ancient farm, which was later renovated by H.D.'s father. From it and onto his parents' land flowed a stream, almost a small river, which flowed onto his parent's land, providing power to various machines and other contraptions.

The Feyer's mill was a rectangular manor with small living quarters, stables, and a barn built round an irresistibly green meadow full of old apple trees. The birthday party took place on that meadow. In the summer of 1917, a friend of the family was living in that relatively primitive house, his Belgian passport having saved him from being drafted. He had sent three reverential invitations, one of which was addressed to His Majesty Hans I, King of Woof Woof (the ten-year-old H.D. was in the habit of expressing his feelings by barking and growling. It is said that back in Cologne one day his mother had been wakened from a nap by loud barking and had moaned: "Oh, that's our Hans out on the street!").

The invitations had been sent by:

The Duchess of Moo-Cow de la Milk—

"As through the grass I chew,
My warmest sentiments I send to you!"

Mrs. Baa-Baa Sheep—

"King Hans of Woof Woof,
For thee my heart doth pound
In all the world thou art
By far the fairest hound!"

And Madame Lisa, the horse—

"I am a democratic mare,
Not pretty, not entrancing
Attend this feast, O King so fair,
There will be lots of prancing!"

Who would have thought that the handwritten invitations would still be remembered seventy-six years later!

The stream, which flowed for about a hundred meters flanked by a path, emptied into in a series of wooded ponds where trout and carp were waiting to be caught. Near these ponds the water ran past the large steel paddlewheel of the mill. Here it supplied all the buildings of the estate with electricity and also pumped drinking water from a nearby well up the hill filling the reservoir that is still in use to this day.

Today, few people remember that the winter of 1917 was one of the coldest on record and that the imperial government had been forced to close schools for a few weeks' "coal vacation." H.D. and his brother went with their governess to stay with the Lange family at the mill. Word went around that the paddlewheel had frozen and that there was only enough electricity left for a few days. Fires were kept going day and night in large iron buckets near the shaft of the paddlewheel, until young and old finally cheered: "The wheel is turning again!"

Soon after the war, H.D.'s parents could again have a car. Its new driver was the same man who had worked for his grandparents. His daughter Gerda accompanied him and became little Freya's playmate (the old driver and his son Hermann had left for Schleswig-Holstein). Franz Bolz, the new driver, remained a close friend of the Deichmann brothers, even after 1931 when everyone had gone their separate ways.

It was in those days that the brothers' car mania began and was egged-on by Bolz's willingness to "let the boys drive," (especially after being plied with a cigar or two from their father's smoking cabinet). At first, they drove back and forth in the Hombusch courtyard. But soon this was no longer enough, and the little driving-zealots got their first real driving experience on the Hombusch-Satzvej road when Bolz drove down to the station on Friday evenings to pick up their father. By now, the price was no longer a cigar but a round of schnapps at the station bar. To throw his father off the scent, H.D. kept his head turned well away from him during the trip home, which didn't do much for the conversation.

Another Hombusch memory that has remained etched in H.D.'s mind was what was called Bolz's afternoon "knitting and crocheting hour," for which the men of the house and sometimes also guests assembled in the courtyard or in Bolz's room to sit about and chat and tell the latest jokes. The knitting and crocheting hour was doubtless a great educational experience for the boys, adding greatly to their independence.

Saying farewell to Hombusch was painful for each family member in different ways. For the children, by now grown up, it meant the final closing of an important chapter of their childhood.

As a memento, their mother took two small thirty-seven centimeter medieval stone lions from the house. They had been a present from her father and had adorned the middle terrace of the house. H.D. inherited them after his mother's death, and they have stood guard ever since in front of the door of his sixth-floor apartment in Milan, ignorant, as H.D. had been until two years earlier, of their symbolic connection to the horse rollers.

December 1993

THE CROCHETED WOOL CAP

In April 1927, knowing little of the world and the unfair distribution of its treasures, H.D. and his friend Rolf Brandt (twenty and twenty-one respectively) set out to study in Vienna for a summer semester. Vienna is a beautiful city, but they knew absolutely nobody there. So they contented themselves with going to two dull lectures each morning and spending the afternoons enjoying the surrounding sights.

Almost two months later, Rolf mentioned quite casually that had been given a letter of introduction to a Dr. Eugenia Schwarzwald (known as "Fraudoktor") who ran a girls' school and had set up four soup kitchens in Berlin in 1923, the worst postwar year in Germany (in Austria at that time it was a little better). One of the soup kitchens was near the university, in a hall of the former Imperial Palace, and Rolf had eaten there as a student. Etta von LeFort, who ran the kitchen, had given him the letter of introduction.

"Rolf! All this time you haven't said a word! Go see her immediately!" Thus browbeaten, Rolf got over his shyness and set out for Wallnerstrasse (Fraudoktor was to tell him later "not to be so very Hamburg" all the time, but he quickly got over that after his first summer in Grundlsee.) He returned perplexed later that day. He had been received a little too warmly he thought (for a Hamburger). Fraudoktor had reproached him for having waited so long before coming to see her and had then rushed out with him into the school hall, which was teeming with girls—it was recess time. "Marion! Ljena!" she had shouted. A few more yells, and suddenly two cheerful and very attractive 18 year-old girls came running. Fraudoktor barked out that this was Rolf, a friend from Berlin, and that the following day they were to go swimming with him in the Danube at Klosterneuburg. Overwhelmed with the sharpness of Fraudoktor's order, and the fact that the girls accepted without batting an eyelash, Rolf had made a quick getaway. H.D. was enchanted with the unexpectedness of the situation. "Two girls is one too many for you to handle," he told Rolf. "I'm coming along!"

Back in those days, one could still swim in the Danube, and the outing was a complete success. Little did the boys know that they were about to begin a lifelong friendship with the girls (Ljena was to marry Rolf's brother Bill, and Rolf, to the end of his days, was to be one of Marion's best friends).

The following day, the girls were called in by Fraudoktor for a report. "Everything went well," they told her. "And his friend is nice too."

"Excellent! Tell them I'm expecting them both for tea tomorrow at Josephstädterstrasse."

Genia and Hermann Schwarzwald lived in a sort of large, one-story pavilion in the back garden at No. 68. It was torn down in the '60s to enlarge the house that stood in front of it. All that remains today of the old structure is the large doorway through which one had to pass to reach the garden. Many a time between 1927 and 1938, H.D. passed through this door, which retains to this day its ornately etched glass paneling. This door, too, would have been a good candidate for a "title-object." With a crocheted wool cap in his bag, he often revisits this memorable door.

When H.D. set foot in this house two days after the swim in the Danube, he could not have imagined that this was to be one of the most decisive steps of his life. But he did realize immediately, without quite knowing how, that fate had decreed that he was about to meet some very special people. Rolf and H.D. were not the only guests there, and out on the street a few hours later Rolf asked H.D. whether he had noticed the very famous people in attendance, among them the writer Egon Friedell with his imposing presence and voice. H.D., so taken with Genia Schwarzwald, had not noticed anyone else.

A few days later, Etta von LeFort arrived from Berlin. Fraudoktor set up a tour of some Viennese community housing for her, and H.D. was allowed to go along. When Etta did not know what to wear to visit these poor families, H.D. suggested, "Dress as simply and as elegantly as you can!" and Fraudoktor, for the first time, gave him a kiss.

The summer vacation began, and Fraudoktor ordered the two German students to come to her summer house on the Grundlsee. It was to be their summer paradise for the next ten years. There life revolved around Fraudoktor for young (H.D.'s contemporaries) and old alike.

Who was Fraudoktor? No one could describe her better than a friend had back in 1926. In the words of Walter Schneider (1897-1970):

> I have seen Eugenie Schwarzwald sparkling with *joie de vivre* on returning from a motoring trip; in utter distress at a mining accident; introducing Knut Hamsun to a class as one introduces an old friend; handling a coffee maker with

childish caution; stamping her foot with indignation at some new case of government corruption. I have heard her passionately singing Schubert's "*Gott in der Natur.*" I have seen her crocheting whimsical wool caps with a passion worthy of higher tasks and glowing with delight as she waved at a trainful of children. I witnessed her comforting young people unhappy in love, poor people filled with despair, old people abandoned; I have seen her pleasure at a new dress, and her indifference at losing a fortune. I saw her tremble before her Russian teacher because she had not done her homework, and I saw her anxiety when, like a schoolgirl late with an essay, she began working on an article for a Sunday newspaper on a Saturday afternoon (far too late). She can dictate three letters, talk on the phone, and hold a meeting simultaneously, and still give her undivided attention to everything with a presence of mind oblivious to both past and future. When she acts on something, she never thinks of the effect it will have: to the critical, objective observer her actions are of an unparalleled purity. How all these conflicting elements can lead to a highly productive and joyful life only she could know, just as only she could know how she managed twenty-five years ago to create a haven of learning in which she could carry out an educational plan based on freedom and joy.

The Seeblick house on the Grundlsee in the Salzkammergut could accommodate every summer—with the help of some of the nearby farms—up to a hundred guests. Genia Schwarzwald at the helm, this was a community "in which no one pretended they were something they weren't, where no one spoke badly of others, and where a tip did not secure one preferential treatment" (Merete Bonnesen, October 29, 1928). There were two special places where we "children" could be with Fraudoktor: at every meal, around the long dinner table on the ground-level open veranda, and up in the attic on the third floor, where Fraudoktor's room was flanked by two small rooms under the eaves where mostly "children" stayed. On evenings when there were no events (concerts, lectures, theater, dancing), we would go up and sit on Fraudoktor's large balcony and talk late into the night about anything and everything. Fraudoktor listened carefully, but spoke only when she was asked a question, or if she disagreed with what was being said, or wanted to add something. On these evenings she would crochet little woolen hats: every "child" had to have his own, and to this end, impromptu fittings— causing great laughter—were necessary.

Today, sixty years later, H.D. still has two of these hats: a black one which he always carries in his bag in case of rain or cold weather, and a green one that he only wears in the country. Beyond their immediate practical use their most important function is that they act as a constant reminder of what the chronicler learned during his thirteen-year friendship with Genia and Hermann Schwarzwald: to listen, to be patient, to avoid prejudice, to be incorruptible in one's judgment, never to gloss over things (a German national affliction); never to lose sight of one's objective and yet not to pursue it at any price; to accept one's mistakes and to acknowledge them; not to take oneself seriously ("self-persiflage," one of Fraudoktor's favorite expressions), to show understanding—for which you need unconditional and yet critical goodwill (H.D. had a full taste of it himself!)—and so much more that a person needs to be free and capable of experiencing "objects" to the fullest.

April 1994

I.D. Cards

Originally only one I.D. card was to appear in this piece—the one that identified H.D. as the director of the de-Nazification tribunal from April 1947 to July 1948. His intention had been to relate some of the experiences at the tribunal which decisively influenced his decision to become an "Adenauer Refugee." But as H.D. went though all his old files looking for this card, many other documents re-surfaced (they are presented at the end of this piece)—documents "attesting" to his activities between 1942 and 1948.

The I.D. card identifying him as a "Representative of The Four-Year Plan," dated March 16, 1942 (exhibit 1), had overnight turned H.D. from a resolutely non-involved civilian into a fully drafted Nazi functionary. Various "object" chapters in this book have dealt with this period.

The Italian I.D. (exhibit 2), issued in Rome where H.D. was stationed, on July 7, 1943, took the place of the previous German card.

The war came to an end for H.D. with his membership in the Italian partisan group, *Giustizia e Libertà* (exhibit 3).

On September 3, 1945, H.D. had returned to Germany (see "Bicycles"), and five days later was issued a "Temporary Registration Card," which also acted as a certificate of discharge for German soldiers (exhibit 3).

Soon after H.D. returned to the void the Nazis had left behind—a total spiritual desert with rubble everywhere—his best friend, Willy Hartner (see "The Chamber Pot of Santa Chiara"), working with the cultural department of the American Army (I.C.D.), asked him to actively help in the rebuilding of the new Germany. Within forty days of his return, H.D. needed a new I.D. that would enable him to get about during curfew hours (exhibit 5).

Why H.D. had to "transport" civilians in his car on November 26, 1945, he can no longer remember (exhibit 6).

Exhibit 7 bears deeply moving memories. This I.D. was arranged for him on December 7, 1945, by some of his American friends at the culture department. It allowed him to take his sister Freya von Moltke and her two small sons from Frankfurt to their mother who was living in Godesberg in the British zone. A British commando had brought Freya to Berlin from Kreisau in Silesia, which had by then become part of Poland. The Americans then flew her from Berlin to Frankfurt and drove her to H.D.'s family at Dornholzhausen in the Taunus. H.D.'s sister-in-law, who was serving in the Dutch military in Berlin, knew that Freya had arrived safely there, but didn't know when or how she would get to H.D.'s. On the evening of November 23, 1945—it was already dark—a military car pulled up outside the house. There was Freya! The last time H.D. had seen her was a year earlier, on November 3, 1944, in Berlin at the Friedrichstrasse station. That was two months before the Nazis tried and then murdered her husband!

The new German I.D. card issued on September 14, 1946 (exhibit 8), is of no real significance, except that one might marvel at the speed with which the Germans went about wiggling their way out of the administrative wasteland the

Nazis left behind. Having been unable to get their hands on new rubber stamps, the officials had simply removed all the swastikas from the old ones.

Exhibit 9: In the aforementioned "The Chamber Pot of Santa Chiara," the chronicler has described his trip to the international philosophers' congress. This precious I.D. had been a form of second passport, allowing German intellectuals (with H.D. as their escort) to attend an international conference for the first time after the war. Securing this I.D. had been an incredibly complicated feat, and no one had known till the very last minute whether it was going to be issued.

Exhibit 10: On November 20, 1946, friends from the Italian resistance in Rome had furnished H.D. (a German obviously not unknown to them!) with a pass to the trial of the Nazi criminals who had shot 335 hostages at the Fosse Ardeatine.

It was only on February 4, 1947, that it was officially attested that H.D. had not been a Nazi, which led to exhibit 11, H.D.'s appointment to the position of supervising chairman of a de-Nazification tribunal, and by extension to exhibit 12, his new "Identification Pass."

H.D.'s friends had asked Walter Hallstein, the new rector of the recently reopened University of Frankfurt, to propose him as a suitable chairman of a special de-Nazification court for generals that was then being set up. The aim of this court was to assure that high-ranking culprits of the Wehrmacht would not be accorded special treatment on account of the still rampant glorification of the German army. (As an example, here is an episode that took place in late October 1946: H.D. was coming from Frankfurt by bicycle and had to get off and push it up a very steep hill. Another man was also pushing his bicycle—he was rather nondescript and wearing tattered clothes typical of 1946. The top Nazi criminals were being sentenced to death at the Nuremberg Trials, among them also Field Marshal Keitel. It wasn't fair, this colorless man argued, that a field marshal who was simply following the Führer's orders should be condemned. H.D. answered that in 1943 he had seen with his own eyes a special order signed by Keitel decreeing that personal belongings of Italian officers shot for refusing to collaborate should be sent to their families with a notification that they had been "killed in action." No more needed to be said, and the two men pushed their bicycles up the hill in silence.) In a curt letter dated January 21, 1948, H.D. was informed that his candidacy for chairmanship of the special de-Nazification court for generals had been denied—"At the present sensitive stage of de-Nazification," the Liberation Minister's letter went, "Dr. Deichmann is indispensable as supervising chairman of the de-Nazification tribunal in the Obertaunus."

H.D.'s hopes for building a real new Germany had been dashed, and this played a large part in his decision to emigrate to Italy. Under the pretense that he was going to work for the American Armed Forces Cultural Department, he and his family finally received a travel permit. This permit was issued on October 26 (see exhibit 13), and eight days later he signed the papers at the mayor's office, canceling his residency in Dornholzhausen (exhibit 14).

On November 5, 1948, H.D. and his family crossed the Italian border at Lake Maggiore, as he noted in his pocket diary.

H.D. will now try to explain to the reader what de-Nazification meant at the time for Germany and for H.D. in particular. Here is a letter that H.D. wrote on August 5, 1948, to a Protestant pastor at Steinbach in the Taunus, in thanks for his kind words concerning H.D.'s chairmanship of the de-Nazification tribunal:

"I have resigned as chairman of the de-Nazification tribunal in the Obertaunus. Looking back, I now realize that I managed to exercise my duties there only to a very limited extent and not in the way I had initially envisioned. The all-out moral and spiritual devastation that Nazism brought with it is so all-encompassing that I must confess, that of all the people I have dealt with in the past fifteen months, very few were seriously concerned with truth and justice. We have received little if any appreciation or encouragement for our efforts. As far as my own culpability is concerned, I feel like you do: I believe that confronting it is the first step towards atonement, and the only way one can hope that the mistakes of the past will not be repeated in the future."

At the direction of the Allied Control Council, on March 6, 1946, the German Federal Court passed the "Liberation from National Socialism and Militarism Act." Nazi party members and everyone else who had voluntarily supported the party—or been coerced into supporting it—were to be classified into five categories (exonerated, collaborator, partially incriminated, fully incriminated, and prime offender) and punished accordingly. The law, however, with its inflexible categories, did little to convince the German people of the importance of a political "cleansing," nor did it convince them that everyone should acknowledge their common responsibility for the horrors committed during the Nazi era. To Germany's detriment, this was never to happen.

In the winter of 1947-1948, H.D. worked hard trying to get the Americans and the Germans to release the large masses of mostly simply foolish "collaborators," and concentrate on the "fully incriminated" and "prime offend-ers." On March 3, 1947, shortly before he was appointed supervising chairman of the de-Nazification tribunal of the Obertaunus, he sent a long letter to the American journalist Dorothy Thompson* concerning the Americans' shortcom-ings, asking her to intercede on his behalf, so that a change in the law could be effected. It was impossible to make amends, he wrote in his letter, if the moral readiness to do so was missing. As there was no such a thing as collective guilt: guilt had to fall on specific individuals, while responsibility had to fall on all. The law, therefore, had to make a sharp distinc-tion between political and economic measures of atonement; limiting the penalty for collaborators of proven political immaturity to a maximum of two thousand reichsmarks was neither morally nor materially feasible. The usufruct concept had to be redefined: individuals who profited from Nazism even without misusing their office should also be considered in this category. The term "exonerated" also had to be redefined (after all, the point was not who had suffered adversity under the Nazis, but who had actually taken personal risks to fight them).

None of H.D.'s objectives met with success. Yet, when H.D., at the urging of the Social Democratic Party, accepted the position of supervising chairman of the de-Nazification tribunal of his district, he did hope to be able to accomplish

---

* (1894-1961) An ardent and clear-sighted anti-Nazi, who had been deported from Germany on Hitler's direct orders. She had been an old friend of both Genia Schwarzwald and H.J. von Moltke. In an obituary in the *Frankfurter Allgemeine Zeitung*, Carl Zuckmayer wrote that she was the "most prominent foreign correspondent the United States has ever had."

something worthwhile, despite the fact that the laws left much to be desired. He was convinced that a political clean-up was absolutely imperative.

In the district of the Obertaunus, 61,374 residents over eighteen years of age had filled out an American questionnaire with one hundred and thirty-one questions. 43,688 were not affected by the law, so the de-Nazification tribunal had to deal only with 17,686 "affected" individuals. After two years, in February 1948, there were still 4,097 cases left. These figures alone offer testimony to the irrationality of this law! In early 1948, after the tribunal's overwhelming experiences, each of the eight chairmen were assigned about thirty more oral cases and a hundred written—the rest were simply given amnesty.

Besides his judiciary duties, the supervising chairman was also responsible for the functioning of the chambers and the distribution of cases. When H.D. had begun working, he had found that judges were selected by a completely illogical alphabetical system, which often led to the defendant being tried by a committee completely unfit for the task. To hinder this miscarriage of justice, H.D. took it upon himself to distribute cases to each judge depending on his intellectual and moral capacity; as a result, he was accused of arbitrariness. H.D. answered to the Liberation Ministry that the only way he could possibly meet the requirements of the law was to distribute cases according to his own conscience. The ministers silently consented.

The crowd stirred when, during his first hearing at the tribunal, H.D. asked for a chair to be brought for the defendant. It was soon understood, however, that his civility in no way affected his condemnation of the crimes of the past. His civility also helped improve the image of the de-Nazification tribunal.

That it had a bad image was unavoidable. At the command of the Americans, a formalistic law had been instituted without anyone telling the German people what the tribunal's objectives were. As a result, the "accused" usually exhibited the worst German national characteristics and very seldom the best.

In general, the defendants lacked both judgment and a sense of responsibility. They were insincere, self-centered, and egotistical, filled with vengeance, greed, cowardice, and brutality. Very few acknowledged their past actions or showed readiness to atone.

Stop! Wait a minute! H.D. almost forgot that he, too, was made to confront these dire German characteristics. In the spring of 1946, the Americans had asked him to become the administrative director of the brand-new Radio Frankfurt. He began work on March 15, 1946, but was fired two months later for being "politically unacceptable."

What had happened?

H.D. had accepted the position with the provision that if he was to be responsible for the administration of Radio Frankfurt, he had to have a say in what was being aired. The German managing director of the station was furious, and went straight to OMGUS in Berlin to alert them that H.D. had held a managerial position (category: "representative") within the Nazi Four-Year plan. Berlin immediately sent word that H.D. was to be fired—there was to be no appeal, regardless of whether it was a technical misapprehension or not. There followed a few months of heated back-and-forth until H.D. finally managed (only with the help of friends who had connections in Washington) to re-establish his reputation as having been one of the few 100% anti-Nazis. He had, however, lost his job at Radio Frankfurt for good.

At many of the hearings, H.D. compared OMGUS's cross-examination tactics to those of the Gestapo—"the only difference is that you leave suspects their fingernails." OMGUS was not amused, and threatened to drag him before the war tribunal if he did not stop spreading "offensive" criticism of the American military government. Here are two typical U.S.-Gestapo statements:

—Major Schaffner had said "We only issue work licenses for the Armed Forces Cultural Department to heroes."

—When H.D. told him that he had just been lucky to have escaped the Gestapo, Professor Bernhard (surely a psychiatrist) told him there was no such thing as luck.

Either way, H.D. was untrustworthy, they claimed, because he had voted for the Communist Party (running under the slogan: "Hitler equals war!") in December 1932, and then in March 1933 for *Zentrum*, the German Catholic Party—the last opposition party to Hitler.

By the end of 1946, OMGUS finally left him alone. It did not, however, formally clear him of Nazism. H.D. accepted the situation, realizing that the unresolved dispute had two sources characteristic of the period: the American victor's ignorance fueled by arrogance, and the misuse of this same shortcoming by the defeated Germans, who were still inextricably enmeshed in their Nazi past. But H.D. did not envision that he would have to submit to three more similar ordeals.

The first ordeal he brought upon himself by requesting that the de-Nazification tribunal issue him a de-Nazification "exemption" notice that would enable him to take over the supervising chairmanship of the tribunal at the request of the

Social Democratic party. He filled out an extensive questionnaire, adding points that anticipated any likely doubts. He
was issued the exemption notice February 4, 1947.

H.D. began work on the de-Nazification tribunal of the
Obertaunus on April 15, 1947. First of all he had to inform
the largely "innocent" defendants targeted by the new laws
of the harsh facts. Some of them were actually innocent, but
H.D. had to convince their accusers of this. What was
usually the hardest part of the job was to persuade plaintiffs,
judges, committee members, and witnesses for the pros-
ecution, not to mention the "liberation minister" that
the aim of the tribunal was not only to ascertain criminality
and seek atonement and possible compensation, but also
to look to the future—in other words, not to push reason to
the side.

Here are some examples of the de-Nazification tribunal's ventures.

—H.D. wrote to the Frankfurt Urban Railway Corporation: "In accordance with the current lifting of the disal-
lowance of employment for former individuals collaborating
with minor Nazi commissions, the defendant must be forth-
with appropriately re-integrated into the work force (punch-
ing tickets instead of laying tracks)!" This "commonsensical"
stance earned H.D. an official reprimand from the Hessian
Liberation Ministry. "Without authority you have challenged
the official judgment passed on the defendant. Should you
undertake such action in the future, formal proceedings will
be brought against you." This threat did not hinder H.D.
from proposing in his rulings that defendants be reinstated
to their former positions as teachers, doctors, judges, county
agents, etc.

—One day H.D. received the following notice from a plaintiff who was also a member of the Social Democratic party: "I wish to inform you of the grave doubts that both I and many of my esteemed colleagues in the party have concerning your lenient handling of certain academics and financiers, i.e., preferential treatment, expedition of their cases, remission of punitive damages." The defendants in question must have been Nazi party members and other formally accused individuals who had, however, demonstrated exemplary behavior in the past twelve years—something that the "formalists" simply could not comprehend.

—Another case that elicited this type of reaction was the case against Prince Wolfgang von Hessen, in which he was "exonerated." For twelve years he had been a party member and a district administrator, coming to the aid of individuals with political or financial problems. Not a single witness accused him of having been a Nazi activist. The same plaintiff who accused the prince of being a sympathizer had shortly before petitioned for the exoneration of the vice-mayor of Oberursel, the prince's protege and comrade-in-arms!

—The proprietor of a tire-tread business, an unobtrusive party member who, however, profited from his Nazi connections, was rightly sentenced by the tribunal as having been a collaborator, while a year later one of his workers, although a known anti-Nazi, was to be given the harsher sentence of "partially incriminated" because he had elicited contributions for the Nazi welfare organization, NSV—as far as the formalists were concerned, a major Nazi organization indeed! For H.D. this was a blatant case of "one law for the rich and another for the poor." He stepped-in himself, as he often did in such cases, as a witness for the defendant with an appeal for "exoneration."

—There was also the case of the "decent" industrialist. He, too, had only been a Nazi party member as a formality, but had, however, on one occasion given a pro-war speech for his firm's sake. This case is mentioned here because the defendant's lawyer was finally asked to determine whether his client was "a sophisticated man of the world," or merely "a victim of political error and Nazi propaganda." Despite his lawyer's idiotic efforts, the sentence passed was "collaborator"—the stickiest part of the case being that all the witnesses called were financially dependent on him.

—H.D. smiled bitterly at the case of a woman who was extremely active as a cell leader in the Nazi Women's Organization. Her sentence read "partially incriminated," and she protested loudly against the fine of four hundred reichsmarks.

—The proprietor of the Diesterweg publishing house was sentenced as "partially incriminated"—many of the Nazi school books he had published were exhibited during the trial. Part of the sentence was that he would not be allowed to work as a publisher for a period of ten years. He appealed, and after H.D. had left his post the publisher, who actually deserved a "fully incriminated" verdict, was downgraded to "collaborator"—he had, after all, "also published so many nice non-political books."

—A certain retired General G., instead of claiming dotage due to lengthy exposure to Nazism, tried instead to pass himself off as an anti-fascist on the grounds that he had never signed up with the Nazi party. Like so many generals of the Third Reich, he declared himself unaware of any crimes his colleagues might have committed as this might to his mind discredit any military honor they might have had left. The General insisted on always being greeted with full official honors—after all he had been personally pensioned by Hitler! One day he was "defamed" by a Nazi party member (how, exactly, is no longer ascertainable). The insulted general demanded satisfaction, and invoked his relationship with Himmler, Kaltenbrunner, and Gauleiter Sprenger. The general only dealt with the elite! He then displayed the photographs of these criminals in his apartment. Even in 1948, he refused to see that he had harmed others and had been under the full influence of the demonic spirit of the times.

H.D. could list countless examples of such de-Nazification cases, which painted a clear picture of the moral situation Hitler left behind.

H.D.'s own case began right before that of General G. For the third time the same foolish accusations were leveled in an attempt to get rid of him. Why did this happen? Why did so many feel H.D. was so troublesome?

In October 1947, while preparing for a case against a former factory security officer of a large industrial concern, information arose that he had mistreated foreign laborers. But the responsible party, the evidence showed, was in actual fact Willi Kunz, now first public prosecutor at the Frankfurt de-Nazification tribunal. He was called as a witness, and on two occasions managed to fabricate reasons under written oath why he could not attend. Not only did the ministry not fire the exposed criminal, but threw H.D. to the Christian Democrats, who managed to launch disciplinary proceedings against him without so much as a preliminary investigation. Even a written complaint from the district representative of the Social Democratic party to the minister on January 12, 1948, fell on deaf ears. Everything pointed to the fact that the minister could be pressured by the Christian Democrats. The disciplinary proceedings turned into preliminary proceedings and ended up at the Frankfurt de-Nazification tribunal as a full charge on November 8, 1948, three days after H.D. had arrived in Italy. The charge made the following ridiculous allegations:

—That H.D. had made a substantial donation to the Nazi Party (in the winter of 1944, H.D. found out that his wife was being harassed by the leader of the local Nazi party for having obtained "domestic help" to which she was not entitled. H.D. offered him a bribe of one hundred reichsmarks, which, on top of everything, for administrative reasons had never been cashed).

—That H.D. had managed to dodge active duty because of his powerful Nazi connections (it is clearly on record, that the G.B. Chem had had him transferred to Berlin for civilian war duty).

—That H.D. had given a speech in praise of fascist Italy at the SA Defense Force, into which he had been conscripted along with all the other men who were not on active duty in Germany. (As "witnesses" have subsequently testified, H.D. had described the pitiful state of the Italian armed forces. "If Hitler had known this . . ." he had said—a purposely daring statement that could well have had dire consequences).

—That H.D. had been Sauckel's representative in Italy, and was therefore responsible for all the laborers—both voluntary and forced—who had been sent from Italy. (H.D. had nothing to do with Sauckel, and had never enlisted a single worker).

For these four groundless accusations, eight Nazi witnesses were called up, none of whom, however, was capable of presenting any actual evidence. Three of them H.D. did not even know.

To top it all off, the liberation minister jumped on the bandwagon and wrote to H.D.: "The disciplinary action [brought against H.D. by Kunz and his Christian Democrat cohorts] has once again brought your political reliability during your employment at I.G. Farben into question, without, however, having directly implicated you. It is questionable, at this point, if your undisciplined comportment makes your continued service as supervising chairman of the de-Nazification tribunal viable." H.D. was called upon to respond under oath but doubted that it meant anything after Willi Kunz's perjury went uncontradicted. Furthermore, H.D. had refused to pass on the case of Fritz Thyssen (the notorious steel magnate who before 1933 had been an important supporter of Hitler, but who in 1944 was thrown into a concentration camp) to a judge who was not of his tribunal—a direct contravention of the law. As far as H.D. was concerned, if the liberation minister wanted to bend the law he would have to go through official channels. "In both these cases," the notification went, "you are addressing direct accusations at the minister in an unforgivable fashion. I am outraged at your comportment, and am herewith issuing an official warning that a repetition of such behavior will mean immediate termination."

This letter was dated March 15, 1948, a little over two months after the minister had assured the rector of the Frankfurt University that H.D. was "indispensable" as supervising chairman of the de-Nazification tribunal in the Obertaunus" to be transferred (exhibit 14). By now the disciplinary action was already in its fortieth day! Unbeknownst to H.D., the minister later brought a case against him to the tribunal in Frankfurt which dragged on until July 22, 1949. The final verdict: case closed, no grounds.

In conclusion, let us laugh a little, but wryly. A Nazi activist wanted to underline his righteousness to the de-Nazification tribunal, and asked a pastor to give him a character reference. The pastor wrote: "I have baptized quite a few of his grandchildren, and have on various occasions sought advice on my heating-unit from this gentleman." (H.D. described the incident in his article "Church and De-Nazification," *Frankfurter Rundschau*, February 7, 1948.) One must learn to live with the fact that the Protestant church had its failings, both during the Hitler era and after it.

February 1995

EXHIBITS

1

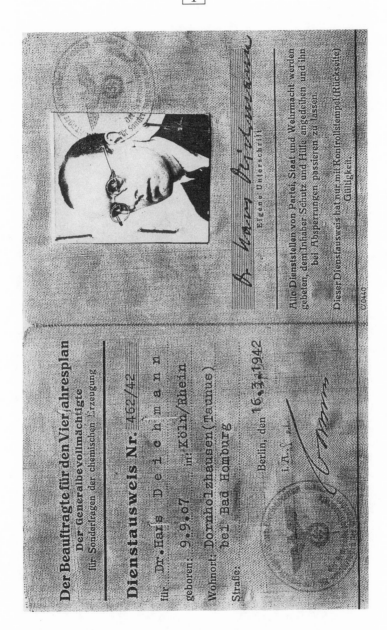

2

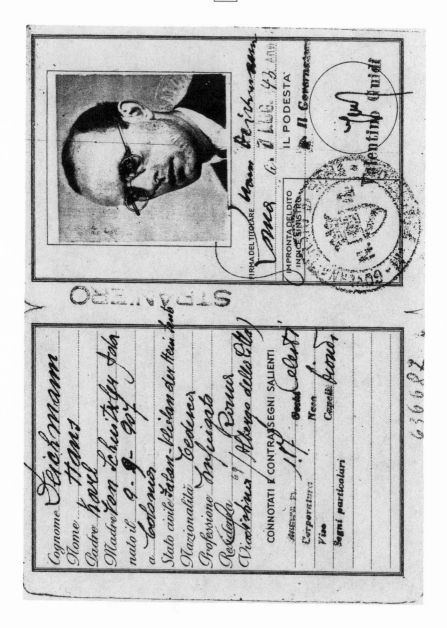

3

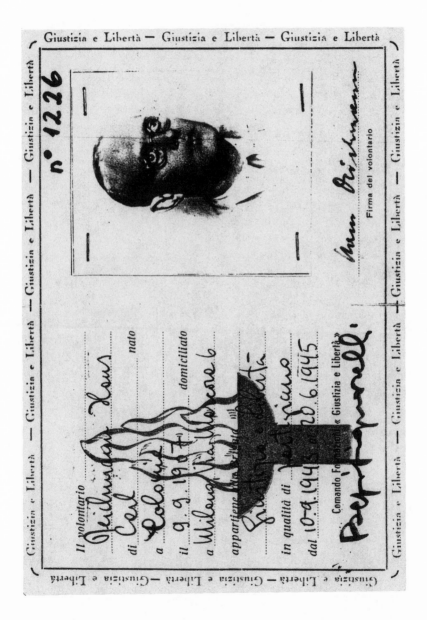

4

MILITARY GOVERNMENT OF GERMANY.

TEMPORARY REGISTRATION.

Zeitweilige Registrierungskarte.

Name   Dr. jur. Deichmann, Hans   Alter 38   Geschlecht männl.
Name   Age   Sex

Ständige Adresse   Darmholzhausen, Ts.   Beruf   kaufm. Angestellter
Permanent Address   Occupation

Jetzige Adresse   Darmholzhausen, Ts. Kammxxxx Oberer - Reisberg
Present Address

Der Inhaber dieser Karte ist als Einwohner von der Stadt   Darmholzhausen, Ts.   vorschrifts-
mäßig registriert und ist es ihm oder ihr strengstens verboten, sich von diesem Platz zu entfernen. Zuwider-
handlung dieser Maßnahme führt zu sofortigem Arrest. Der Inhaber dieses Scheines muß diesen Ausweis stets
bei sich führen.

The holder of this card is duly registered as a resident of the town of   Darmholzhausen, Ts.   and is
prohibited from leaving the place designated. Violation of this restriction will lead to immediate arrest.
Registrant will at all times have this paper on his person.

Charles A. Kramer
Capt. FA

Name and Rank
Mil Gov Officer, U. S. Army

Datum der Ausstellung
Date of Issue

8.9.45.

Druck: C. Zeuner & Co., Bad Homburg

Entlassungschein.

Legitimations - Nummer
Identity Card Number

Hans Deichmann

Unterschrift des Inhabers
Signature of Holder

Right Index Finger

(Dies ist kein Personal-Ausweis und erlaubt keine Vorrechte.)
(This is not an identity document and allows no privileges.)

5

STRATEGIC SERVICES UNIT, GERMANY
UNITED STATES FORCES
EUROPEAN THEATER

APO 757
November 26, 1945.

TO WHOM IT MAY CONCERN

    Mr. Deichmann, Dornholzhausen, near Bad
Homburg, is hereby authorized to transport civilians
between Wiesbaden and Dornholzhausen, near Bad Homburg,
after curfew, on the 26th of November 1945.

Edwin F. Black

Edwin F. Black,
Lt.Col., GSC.

6

MILITARY GOVERNMENT - GERMANY
Militär-Regierung - Deutschland
DETACHMENT 12 D2   № 007346

NAME: Dr. Hans Deichmann
Name:

IDENTITY CARD: MG Registration Card
Ausweiskarte:

IS AUTHORIZED TO TRAVEL WITHIN THE FOLLOWING AREA:
ist befugt innerhalb des folgenden Gebietes zu reisen:

Curfew Exemption for duties

REASON: official work for ICD U.S.F.E.T.
Grund:

VALID FROM 15 October 45 TO 1 December 45
Gültig von   bis

Capt.

MGO

Extension No. 1
Extended to 1 February 46

A. L. YAKOUBIAN
Capt. CAC
MGO

Extension No. 2
Extended to 30 April 46

OLIVER C. KUNTZLEMAN
AUS
Captain
MGO

Extension No. 3

212

7

r/MG/PS/G 6

GOUVERNEMENT MILITAIRE EN ALLEMAGNE
*MILITARY GOVERNMENT OF GERMANY

MILITÆRREGIERUNG - BEFREIUNG   205838 ✳
DISPENSE ACCORDÉE PAR LE
GOUVERNEMENT MILITAIRE
MILITARY GOVERNMENT EXEMPTION
A.M.F.A. No.

Datum der Ausstellung ___ Wird unwirksam am ___ 31.1.46
Date de l'établissement   Expires on
Date Issued
Name ___ Dickmann, Hans
Nom
Name
Anschrift ___ Wohnort ___ parts ___
Adresse   Lieu
Address   Towit.
Ausweiskarte Klasse ___ P.P. Nr. ___ E 10141
Identity Card Type   No.
Unterschrift des Inhabers ___ Hans Dickmann
Sign.   du détenteur
Signature of Holder

ANWEISUNGEN: Diese Befreiung ist im Namen der Militärregierung
ausgestellt worden, darf nicht verändert, ist nicht übertragbar, darf nicht abgeändert
oder vernichtet werden und ist nur gültig in Verbindung mit der
Ausweiskarte des Inhabers. Der Verlust dieser Karte muss der Polizei
gemeldet werden. Gefundene oder unwirksam gewordene Karten
müssen der ausstellenden Behörde zurückgegeben werden.
INSTRUCTIONS: Cette carte a été accordée par le Gouvernement
Militaire, elle ne peut être transmise, ni modifiée, ni détruite et
n'est valable qu'avec la carte d'identité du titulaire. La perte
de la carte d'identité doit être signalée à la Police. Toute carte trouvée, ou
rendue non valable doit être retournée à l'autorité qui l'a délivrée.
INSTRUCTIONS: This is issued by Military Government. It is not
transferable and must not be altered or destroyed, and is only valid when used
in conjunction with holder's identity card. The loss of this card must
be reported. If found, or on expiration of validity, this card
must be returned to the issuing authority.

GRUENDE, EINZELHEITEN UND AMTLICHE UNTERSCHRIFT:
Die umstehend benannte Person ist, wie unten angegeben, von Be-
schränkungen betreffend: AUSGANG — REISE — VERBOTENE
GEGENSTÄNDE — SPERRBEZIRK befreit. (Nicht zutreffendes
ist durchzustreichen.)

MOTIFS, PARTICULARITÉS ET SIGNATURE OFFICIELLE: La
personne désignée au verso a obtenu la présente dispense unique-
ment pour être dispensée des restrictions spéci fiées ci-après:
COUVRE-FEU — VOYAGE — OBJETS PROHIBÉS — ZONES
INTERDITES (Rayer les mentions inutiles.)

REASONS, SPECIFICATIONS AND ENDORSEMENTS: The person
named on the reverse hereof is granted exemption, only as specified
below, from restrictions respecting: CURFEW — TRAVEL — PRO-
HIBITED ARTICLES — PROHIBITED AREA (delete where applicable.)

USE OF BRIDGES AND FERRIES   permit de traverser les ponts

EINZELHEITEN DER BEFREIUNG
DÉTAILS CONCERNANT LA DISPENSE
PARTICULARS OF EXEMTION

GRUENDE:
MOTIFS:
REASONS:

Auth. to circu-   Wiesbaden–Bonn–Köln–
late between
autorisé de circuler entre

travel by order of Information
Control Division / voyage officielle

Ausstellende Behörde   Mil Govt det F 15
Administration ayant autorisé la dispense
Issuing Organisation

Name (in block) ___ H. LENNEVILLE   CAPT. AUS
Nom   Rank

Unterschrift ___ Stammnr.
Signature   No. Matric. 0634065
Signature: MIL. GOVT.   Serial No.

A. Kindermann - Mainz

8

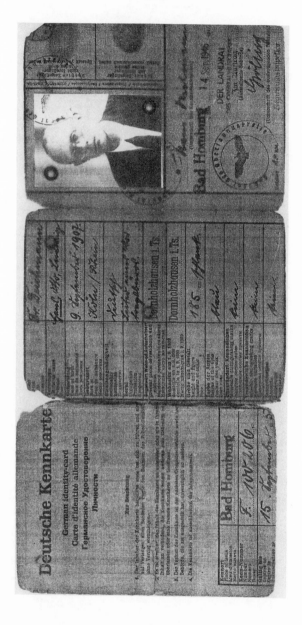

9

10

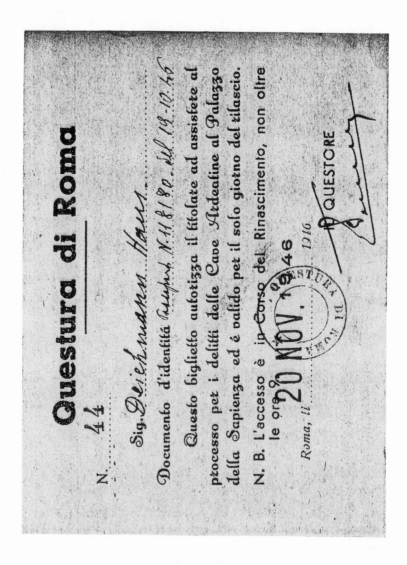

Questura di Roma

N. 44

Sig. Deichmann Hans

Documento d'identità Passport N.11 8180 del 19.10.46

Questo biglietto autorizza il titolare ad assistere al
processo per i delitti delle Cave Ardeatine al Palazzo
della Sapienza ed è valido per il solo giorno del rilascio.

N. B. L'accesso è in Corso del Rinascimento, non oltre
le ore 9°

20 NOV. 1946

Roma, lì 1946

QUESTORE

11

HESSISCHES STAATSMINISTERIUM
     Der Minister
für politische Befreiung

Wiesbaden, den 18.April 1947

E r n e n n u n g

Herr Dr.Hans D e i c h m a n n
wird hiermit auf Grund meiner "Dienstordnung für die
öffentlichen Kläger und die Spruch- und Berufungs-
kammern" vom 21.Januar 1947 (Amtsblatt Nr. 4 vom
29.1.1947) zum
     dienstaufsichtsführenden Vorsitzenden

der Spruch - Berufungs-Kammer   Obertaunus
     mit der Bezeichnung

  "Dienstaufsichtsführender Vorsitzender"

ernannt.

Die besonderen Aufgaben des "Dienstaufsichtsführenden
Vorsitzenden" sind in der o.a.Dienstordnung festge-
legt.

Die Vertrauenszulage regelt sich nach den Bestimmungen
der Rundverfügung. Nr. 42 Abs.VII vom 7.11.1946.

Diese Ernennung ist jederzeit widerruflich.

(B i n d e r)

12

An alle zu... idigen militärischen u. zivilen Dienststellen:

Der Träger dieses Ausweises ist vom deutschen Ministerium sorgfältig ausgewählt und von der Mil. Reg. als Beauftragter zur Vollstreckung des Gesetzes zur Befreiung vom National-Sozialismus und Militarismus genehmigt worden. Er untersteht nicht der Sperrstundenvorschrift und im Bedarfsfall ist ihm sofortige Hilfe zu seinem persönlichen Schutz oder zur Ausübung seines Dienstes zu gewähren.

TRIBUNAL
(SPRUCHKAMMER)

IDENTIFICATION PASS

OFFICE OF MILITARY GOVERNMENT
FOR GREATER HESSE

IDENTIFICATION

18.4.47   No 3096

Attention: All Military and Civilian Law Enforcement Agencies:

The bearer of this card has been carefully selected by the German Ministry and approved by Military Government as an "Official Carrying Out the Law for Liberation from National Socialism and Militarism". He ... be exempt from curfew regulations and ... immediate. Assistance whenever ... required for his protection or carrying ... his duties.

Office of Military Government
Greater Hesse

OFFICIAL
Liaison and Security
Kreis Oberteure...

NAME _Dr. Hans DEICHMANN_
ADDRESS _Dornholzhausen, Am oberen Reisberg_
BIRTHDATE _9.9.07_
SIGNATURE _Hans Deichmann_

13

OFFICE OF MILITARY GOVERNMENT FOR HESSE   tt
Education and Cultural Relations Division
APO 633   US Army

Wiesbaden, Germany
26 October 1948

184.29

SUBJECT: **Exit Permit for Mr. and Mrs. Deichmann**

TO   : **Dr. Hans Deichmann**
          Dornholzhausen (Obertaunus),Am oberen Reisberg

          This is to notify you that your travel docu-
ment has been issued and can be picked up at this office.
Office hours are Monday to Friday from 0830 to 1200 and
1300 to 1730 hours.

                                    VAUGHN R DELONG
                                    Deputy Director

Tel: Wiesbaden Civ 59231
Ext: 408
Room: 319

14

Der Bürgermeister . Dornholzhausen (Ts.), den ....3.11.......... 194 8

Dornholzhausen (Ts.)

Tg.B.Nr. _____ An _____

Betr: Reiseabmeldung.

Herr Dr. Hans Deichmann und folgende Familienangehörige

meldeten sich heute auf Reisen ab.

Dr. Hans Deichmann	geb.	9.9.07.
Senta Deichmann	„	27.8.12.
Maria Deichmann	„	13.9.36.
Thomas Deichmann	„	11.5.38.
Mathias Deichmann	„	11.7.43.

Sie sind mit Lebensmittelkarten bis zum 30.11.1948 versorgt.

Langfristige Karten sind nicht im Besitz.

Der Bürgermeister.